TREASURE CHEST II

Problem-Solving Activities, Brain Stretchers, and Active Games,

by Karynne L. M. Kleine

National Middle School Association
Westerville, Ohio

NMSA is a registered servicemark of National Middle School Association.

Printed in the United States of America.

Betty Edwards, Executive Director
April Tibbles, Director of Publications
Carla Weiland, Publications Editor
John Lounsbury, Editor, Professional Publications
Mary Mitchell, Designer, Editorial Assistant
Dawn Williams, Publications Manager
Lindsay Kronmiller, Graphic Designer
Jonathan Starr, Graphic Designer
Marcia Meade-Hurst, Senior Publications Representative
Peggy Rajala, Publications & Event Marketing Manager
Amanda Hall, Photographer

Library of Congress Cataloging in Publication Data
Kleine, Karynne L. M. (date)
 Treasure chest II : problem-solving activities, brain stretchers, and active games /
by Karynne L. M. Kleine.
     p. cm.
 Includes bibliographical references.
 ISBN 978-1-56090-231-7
 1. Middle school education--United States. 2. Middle school education--Activity programs--United States. 3. Child development--United States. I. Title.
 LB1623.5.K48 2009
 373.1102--dc22

                         2009031685

National Middle School Association
4151 Executive Parkway, Suite 300
Westerville, Ohio 43081
1-800-528-NMSA   f: 614-895-4750
www.nmsa.org

Contents

Can You Identify
With These Thoughts?

The world of today's adolescent is full of irony—Corey is enveloped by media so that even when he is isolated, he is continually influenced by others. Julie finds herself sending dozens of text messages per day, with an immediate response expected so that, not surprisingly, her sense of time becomes warped and reflection is held at bay. Then there is Henri, who sits tap-tap-tapping on the computer waiting six seconds for an Internet search to be completed; and by observing his aggravated bearing, I think he feels an eternity must have passed. As the pace of life continually increases, with scheduling and activities the norm rather than the exception, self-directed "free time" has morphed into a theoretical premise for many middle schoolers rather than an actual construct. But at the opposite extreme is that occasional youngster such as Martha, who has nothing but "free time" because of so little meaningful interaction with others that no activity seems worthy of her pursuit. With such realities, even the more determined youth can find themselves sidetracked by a multitude of distractions with little guidance on how to meet their potential.

Paradoxically, this seesawing from hurly-burly to ennui abounds precisely as middle school students are faced with decisions that have long-term and life-changing significance. Young adolescents are undergoing wide-ranging and dramatic—often seemingly traumatic—changes just in time to heighten the risks associated with the numerous and mounting pressures they experience. They go through more rapid and overall modification than at any other period of life. If you added six inches and 40 pounds to your frame over the course of a year, and if your thinking patterns were undergoing alterations while you were trying to decide if you were ever going to talk to your best friend again, insecurity and idiosyncrasy would be your constant companions.

Changes just this extensive are typical of youth in the middle grades. When coupled with the external demands presented by the contemporary world, without some intervention many adolescents will be ill-equipped to understand, let alone to deal with the simultaneous swell of self and world change. A veteran middle school teacher expressed an important reality when she declared: "Kids today may be the same as we were when I was that age, but the consequences of their behavior are different—and frightening."

If you identified with these thoughts and have already recognized what an anxious period adolescence is for many young people, especially in these precipitous times with the relentless focus on standardized tests in schools, you are probably searching for ways to address their personal-social development. Anxious not to slight the academic needs of adolescents, but wanting to increase their self-confidence, their ability to see the world through others' eyes, their collaborative and social proficiency, their decision-making skills, and their perseverance and competence, you seek ways to achieve these non-academic but critically important goals. While we all wait for the realignment of social forces that are buffeting today's young adolescents, we can and do turn to a stable institution that can assist young adolescents—the middle school—for it can and does provide the help youth need as they mature and become responsible young adults.

What's In This Book for You?

Whether you are a member of an interdisciplinary team, an exploratory teacher, a special education teacher, a counselor, or an advisor, there is real help for you in this resource. This sequel to National Middle School Association's popular *Treasure Chest: A Teacher Advisory Source Book* (Hoversten, Doda, & Lounsbury, 1991) offers a wide array of activities, games, brain stretchers, and problems that will help you get students engaged, build relationships, keep them moving, and foster the development of the all-important people skills. These activities are particularly useful in meeting many of the behavioral objectives of middle level education that are hard to "get at" through regular classroom instruction. That the intellectual development of young adolescents is the prime responsibility of the middle school is a given, but it is not its only responsibility. The middle school movement has been unapologetically committed to assisting youth in their overall development, and necessarily so; for, indeed, the whole young adolescent does come to school; and as Richard Lipka (1997) has reminded us: "Cognitive learning is hard-won by someone whose life is in affective disarray" (p. 37).

The middle school movement has thus advanced programs and practices that offer assistance to 10- to 15-year-olds in growing up physically, socially, emotionally, morally, as well as intellectually. Middle grades teachers have regularly used special activities (such as these) to open the door for dealing with the personal-social needs of young adolescents. Such activities often also provide for the much-needed physical movement and lead to the desired easy but honest banter among students. Not to be overlooked, however, are both the direct and the indirect contributions that these activities make toward the academic and intellectual growth of students. Recent research studies have made clear the value of physical movement and games to intellectual development.

The activities included in this resource are indeed varied. They range from ones that are just-for-fun to ones that seriously challenge the intellect of all. Some focus on a particular skill, while others focus on knowledge acquisition. There is no set pattern or sequence for the use of these activities. It is essential that you become familiar with the activities and have them sufficiently in the back of your mind so when an occasion arises that would be well-served by a certain activity, you will recall it and turn to this resource.

Activities in Section One, for the most part, are useful in the early part of the school year as teachers try to build a learning community; but some of these activities could and should be used intermittently throughout the year as a pick-me-up or as a rainy day activity and not be related to the ongoing study. With each activity, an amount of time it will take to complete is indicated, but it is a guess. Often when an activity is successful, students will suggest repeating it with a better or quicker variation. Many of the activities also call for follow-ups; and some will lead to investigations that become significant academic learning experiences. As always, the leader's judgment and understanding of the group help determine how much discussion to encourage and when to end an activity. The group's status as a team or a bonded community will determine much about how long an activity takes, or, in fact, if it is even an appropriate one for this group. The leader's professional judgment is the main guide.

And so it goes; there is no curriculum here, rather a collection of special activities for teachers, teams, or advisors to draw from at their discretion to serve a specific objective or meet a recognized need.

For advisors

The activities here can provide a substantial portion of the curriculum for advisory programs. Middle schools instituted advisory programs in large numbers in the 70s to specifically advance the personal-social development of students. Such programs have struggled, but their existence remains a recommendation in the literature. In fact, NMSA's recent revision of *This We Believe* (2010) states: "Every young adolescent's academic and personal development is guided by an adult advocate. . . . Each middle level student must have one adult in the school who assumes special responsibility for supporting that student's academic and personal development" (p. 35).

Advisory programs, nevertheless, have admittedly had difficulty becoming fully operational. Programs may have been initiated too quickly without adequate faculty buy-in or preparation and were soon dropped. Sometimes programs lacked a sufficient focus or a meaningful curriculum. And, quite honestly, they often met with considerable faculty resistance. Many teachers who viewed themselves as qualified instructors in a subject did not feel they should or could be responsible for what appeared to be more the responsibility of guidance counselors. Yet, advisory programs when properly instigated are most effective in achieving some of the important goals of middle level education that are hard to meet in the standard academic curriculum of separate subjects. There are indications that advisory programs are undergoing a renaissance.

If you plan to use activities in this handbook as you initiate or reinvigorate an advisory program, first seek the support of the entire faculty and administration; experience has shown that any program launched without full faculty support is an accident waiting to happen.

National Middle School Association has several publications to assist you with advocacy and advisories. The first, *Launching a Successful Advisory Program* (Niska & Thompson, 2007), is a "sure-fire, can't go wrong" resource that a school definitely will want to use when implementing an advisory program—or when seeking to revive a dying or struggling program. Designed as a do-it-yourself professional development kit, this resource will take an entire faculty or a team through a thoughtful study of advisory programs and end up with a specific plan for a program that involved all the participants in its development. The kit contains all the materials needed to complete the tasks that are in the nine modules. In addition, an accompanying DVD of video clips from real schools gives face and voice to the various topics discussed. Frankly, it is hard to conceive of a school's starting an advisory program without taking advantage of this practical resource.

A second, related NMSA publication is *Taking the Lead in Implementing and Improving Advisory* (Spear, 2005). One of the titles in the Middle Level Leadership Series, this brief, practical resource, which touches all aspects of advisory, offers guidance to the administrator or other leaders responsible for directing the development and implementation of an advisory program.

A third publication to consider is *Teaming and Advisory: Perfect*

Partners (Rottier, Woulf, Bonetti, & Meyer, 2009), which presents a model that merges advisory with teaming. The model is described fully and then illustrated with the actual implementation of the model at DePere Middle School in Wisconsin. It is based on the belief that where teams are operating successfully, they can readily assume responsibility for a struggling advisory program, and both teaming and advisory will benefit from such a merger.

A fourth book that warrants consideration is *From Advisory to Advocacy: Meeting Every Student's Needs* (James & Spradling, 2001). Here is a passionate plea for establishing in middle schools a "culture of compassion and advocacy" and not relying on an independent advisory program to fulfill a middle school's responsibility for advocacy. This publication includes examples and activities to make its case.

References

Hoversten, C., Doda, N., & Lounsbury, J. (1991). *Treasure chest: A teacher advisory source book.* Columbus, OH: National Middle School Association.

Lipka, R. (1997). Enhancing self-concept/self-esteem in young adolescents. In J. Irwin (Ed.), *What current research says to the middle level practitioner* (p. 37). Columbus, OH: National Middle School Association.

James, M., & Spradling, N. (2001). *From advisory to advocacy: Meeting every student's needs.* Westerville, OH: National Middle School Association.

National Middle School Association. (2010). *This we believe: Keys to educating young adolescents.* Westerville, OH: Author.

Niska, J., & Thomson, S. (2007). *Launching a successful advisory program.* Westerville, OH: National Middle School Association.

Rottier, J., Woulf, T., Bonetti, D., & Meyer, E. (2009). *Teaming and advisory: Perfect partners.* Westerville, OH: National Middle School Association.

Spear, R. (2005). *Taking the lead in implementing and improving advisory.* Westerville, OH: National Middle School Association.

Activities Galore

As Ross Burkhardt has noted in his most engaging book, *Inventing Powerful Pedagogy: Share, Steal, Revise, Own* (2009), teachers have been notorious thieves, acquiring ideas to use in their classrooms whenever and wherever they found them. And so it is with the activities compiled in this resource; they came—were stolen, if you will—from many sources and individuals. While I have adapted and altered them, few, if any, are my creations. Several of them are adaptations of old familiar activities, such as the Coat of Arms used here with a different spin. In some cases, an original source is known and cited, but for the most part these activities reside in that teacher's version of the public domain. All of these activities have been used in middle level schools with young adolescents.

The activities are organized in ways that will help you select an appropriate one. First, they are organized in three broad categories: 1. physical development, 2. cognitive development, and 3. social and emotional development.

Physical development activities involve physical movement and often require being outside. They are particularly useful in building relationships, getting to know one another, and establishing trust; but two involve lessons on health issues.

Cognitive development activities involve problem solving, decision making, mind-stretching games, and puzzles that call for some serious thinking.

The **social and emotional activities** section covers a variety of areas from developing leadership skills to listening skills, from behaving responsibly to service-learning.

As you will quickly see when you review the activities, these three divisions are anything but clear-cut. Almost all of the activities actually relate to cognitive development in some way, and most of those in the cognitive development category involve some physical movement and include an element of socialization. The plea for you to develop a familiarity with all the activities bears repeating.

The activities are also organized rather loosely in another way. Those activities that are easiest to carry out are placed toward the front of each section, while the ones that are more involved, requiring some skills or knowledge from the leader and likely to take longer are located toward the back part of the section. In addition, each activity is keyed with a symbol or two to help you quickly grasp its nature and function.

The time factor often presents a dilemma for an advisory group that has a 20–30 minute scheduled period; but for a team with a block of time at its disposal, springboards to further learning that occur can be used to full advantage. Some of the most meaningful discussions about serious issues regularly evolve from these activities. Relevancy is usually present as is engagement, providing the two most desired characteristics for a valuable learning experience.

Reference

Burkhardt, R. (2009). *Inventing powerful pedagogy: Share, steal, revise, own.* Westerville, OH: National Middle School Association.

Physical Development

Active, motor development, outdoor, health-related activities

The activities in this section for the most part focus on getting participants moving, often outside the classroom. Others involve the consequences of decisions students make regarding long-term health and well-being. These activities are good for team building, getting everyone better acquainted, developing students' social skills, and learning new concepts. While many of them would be used as teams and groups are first becoming established, using some of them periodically throughout the year makes sense.

Legend: **A** activities that can be completed quickly, are active, and fun

L activities that are less physically taxing

O activities that lend themselves to the outdoors or open areas

S activities that require strategizing or developing skills

1. Chain Tag ▣ ◙

Purpose: Just for plain, old-fashioned fun and to get some energy flowing through the body.

Materials: No materials necessary.

Time: 10–20 minutes.

Directions: Gather outside or in a large, open space. One person is selected as the "chaser" and another is selected to be "it." Other participants are divided into groups of 3–4 persons. These small groups link arms to form small chains. The game proceeds as normal tag, except the person who is "it" and is being chased can "link-up" with any small group. This frees the person on the other end of that small chain to become "it." This sets the chaser after a new "it" and enhances the fun and uncertainty. The chaser can "link-up" and insert a fresh chaser into the game.

One of the benefits of chain tag is that it encourages participation even from those who are not particularly athletic, as no one has to run for a long period of time. Cheering for an "it" is permissible. Terminate the game when it seems to have run its course—just a matter of judgment.

2. Whoosh ▣

Purpose: To involve all in a fast and fun game that calls for cooperation.

Materials: No materials necessary.

Time: 5–15 minutes

Directions: Standing in a circle, participants orally pass the word
               "whoosh" around from one person to another. The
               activity moves rapidly, building and sustaining community
               involvement. The leader can suggest variations, including
               switching directions, sending multiple whooshes at one time
               while standing shoulder to shoulder or at arm's length, and
               keeping the circle moving clockwise. Timing the activity
               motivates improvement as does standing in shapes other than
               a circle, such as overlapping figure eights.

3. Apple Cart ▲

Purpose: To have fun, sharpen everyone's attention, and release energy.

Materials: A chair for each participant, minus one.

Time: 10–15 minutes

Directions: The group sits in a circle on chairs, with one person left standing in the middle. Participants are equally divided between three fruits (such as apples, oranges, and bananas) scattered among the group. When the middle person calls out a fruit (e.g., "apples"), all the apples move to change chairs, with the middle person then able to claim an open chair. The person left without a chair becomes the next caller. If, after three or four rounds a caller says "apple cart," everyone has to change chairs.

Between rounds, the caller may provide a rest beak by making an impromptu one-minute speech or sharing something learned in a recent class. Students may volunteer to make such talks; or knowing the members well, the caller may ask someone to do this.

4. Orbit Toss A O

Purpose: To provide physical movement for all in a competitive activity
              that involves a bit of dexterity.

Materials: Three increasingly wider spherical objects are needed to
              form a target on the floor in the center of a large area. A
              tire, a hula-hoop, and lengths of rope work well for forming
              the target. Also needed are at least three soft balls for each
              participant, or at least for half the group. These can be
              purchased or made out of yarn or rolled socks. Students may
              procure these on their own from home.

Time: 20–30 minutes

Directions: Divide the players into two teams, A and B. Members of Team
              A encircle the target and jog clockwise while raising their
              hands to block shots. The members of Team B are positioned
              outside of Team A and have three soft balls each. Team B jogs
              counterclockwise while attempting to toss the balls into the
              target. When everyone's balls have been thrown, the score is
              tallied. Team B earns one point for each ball in the outermost
              circles, three for each in the middle circle, and five for the
              innermost circle. Then the teams choose positions, and Team
              A tries to score more points. Awkward motions and errant
              pitches usually produce laughs.

5. Pass It On ▲ ●

Purpose: To work out excess energy while developing dexterity and
                teamwork.

Materials: At least 10 hula hoops.

Time: 5–30 minutes, depending on rounds played.

Directions: Participants form two teams of equal number. The teams face
                one another and interlock their hands, forming a long chain.
                The hoops are stacked next to the first student who begins the
                chain using his free hand to start each hoop down the line.
                The teams must pass all of their hoops from one to another
                without breaking hand grips and stack them next to the
                person who is the final member of the chain. The first team to
                complete the activity wins!

Follow-up: The groups can discuss the challenge of maintaining
                connections during the activity and relate this to effective
                teamwork. In second or third rounds, lessons learned become
                evident as observation and experience pay off.

6. Hands Free ⬛s⬛ ⬛o⬛

Purpose: To improve dexterity and build awareness of others.

Materials: One ball for each participant—minus one. Use soft balls, such as Nerf™ balls. The balls may be different sizes.

Time: If the game is played several times with strategizing between rounds, the game can go on for 20 or more minutes.

Directions: Students line up and hold hands facing a wall in an unobstructed area such as a gym or field. A leader places a ball between the shoulders of every student and the next person. The object of the game is to walk in a group and transfer as many balls as possible to a designated area. Points are awarded for each ball that reaches the area without being dropped.

Follow-up: The groups can discuss the challenge when using balls of various sizes for the activity and relate this to flexible response to change.

7. Out of Step ▪

Purpose: To develop agility and creativity and have fun.

Materials: No materials or equipment necessary.

Time: 10 minutes.

Directions: Participants are paired off and face one another. They remove their shoes and join hands. At the "start" signal, each person attempts to step softly on the toes of the other, counting aloud at any successful contact. The first person to reach 10 wins the game. A second or third round can be done with new partners and then possibly with someone challenging the winners as the rest of the group becomes an audience.

8. How About It? ▪A ▪O

Purpose: To get folks moving! Plan in advance for participants to wear suitable clothes. The point is to put a twist on movements that generally take place in a routine manner.

Materials: This can be played with no materials, but the activity can be enhanced with balls, ropes, blindfolds, poles, or other equipment. A stopwatch and a ruler should also be available.

Time: 30 minutes.

Directions: The leader can start by offering challenges; then others can take the lead and offer alternative movements. If you have jump ropes, balls, or other equipment, you can extend the challenges.

How quickly can you get from point A to point B? How quickly can you do it on your hands and knees? Backwards?

How long can you hop on one foot? Jump rope? Bounce a ball?

How far can you toss a Nerf™ ball? With your "wrong" hand?

How smoothly can you zigzag through a space? Blindfolded?

How high can you reach? Sitting down? With a beanbag atop your head?

How low can you limbo? How low can you limbo holding hands with a partner?

9. Making Progress ▣ ◙

Purpose: To encourage students to be creative in their movements.

Materials: An open area, field, or gym is needed for this quick game.

Time: 20 minutes.

Directions: Participants stand behind a line. Each in turn must cover the space between the starting line and another line about 20 or so yards distant, using a different form of locomotion than any of the previous players. For example, the first one called upon to cover the distance between the lines walks, the second one skips, the third hops, the fourth crawls, the fifth walks backward, and so on until all of the players have reached the far line. This game calls for the last players to be ingenious, as they have to initiate new methods of progressing. You can change this by lining up the group all at once and telling members to cover their eyes and then start. Any participants using the same form of locomotion must drop out until just one is left or you've played several rounds.

10. Really Fun Relay ▣ ▣

Purpose: To encourage students to be quick in their movements.

Materials: An open area, such as a gym or a ball field, something to
                mark circles, and two small, identical objects, such as
                magic markers.

Time: 15 minutes or more.

Directions: Participants count off and divide themselves into two equal-
                numbered groups, with each group forming a straight line by
                ascending height. Opposite and at about 50 and 60 feet in
                front of the first player in each line, mark two circles (about
                eight inches in diameter) on the ground, one about ten feet
                behind the other. In the nearest of each of the circles place
                a small object such as a marker. When you say "Go," the first
                player of each line runs to the first circle, grabs the marker,
                and places it in the second circle, ten feet off. She then races
                back and touches the outstretched hand of the next player
                in the line. Once she makes contact with the next person in
                the relay she moves to the back of her team's relay line. The
                second player, when touched, races to the marker, and in the
                same way, places the item back in the closer circle, returning
                to tap the hand of the next player in her line. This continues
                until each player of the line has had her turn. The last player,
                having deposited the marker in the circle, returns to the line,
                touching the outstretched hand of the first in line. If the teams
                are unequal, the leader can participate, or a participant can
                be used to help referee the game.

11. Blanket Ball □ s

Purpose: To demonstrate the need for cooperating and
               communicating to accomplish a goal.

Materials: A sheet or blanket. The game can be played in a gym or
               outside if there is a basketball goal on site.

Time: 20 minutes for several rounds.

Directions: This fun and challenging activity can be played with groups of
               two or four. The task is for each small group to hold the blanket
               taut and see how many baskets it can make in a particular
               time period by thrusting the ball with the blanket. No hands
               can touch the ball.

12. Great Feat ◙

Purpose: To blow off steam or unwind.

Materials: Each player needs one beanbag to begin. Appoint a referee
                to help monitor time and adherence to the rules.

Time: 20 minutes or so.

Directions: Before this active game begins, agree upon a penalty stunt,
                such as a cartwheel or one minute of jogging in place.
                Students each with a beanbag spread out over the open but
                established playing area. When the signal is given, players
                "bowl" their beanbags toward the feet of other players, who
                attempt to dodge the contact. The beanbag is kept low as
                the object is to hit feet only. If a player gets hit in the feet he
                must go to the penalty box and perform whatever penalty
                stunt has been established before rejoining the game. A
                player can't be hit again while performing the stunt. Any
                beanbags on the ground are free for any player to take and
                use.

13. Korny Kickball ◙

Purpose: To provide for the active involvement of teams with minimal emphasis on competition.

Materials: Five bases set around the perimeter of a large but defined area and a kickball.

Time: 30 minutes.

Directions: In addition to the number of bases, what distinguishes this from traditional kickball is that players do not have to run but may wait as long as they care to on a base. However, when they do decide to run to another base, they must join hands with any other teammates already on that base and stay linked together when they try for the next base. Outs are made by catching the ball or tagging any one of a group of runners. Tagging any one, or several, of a group of runners only counts as one out.

14. Digit, Get-It A L S

Purpose: To improve motor skills and promote discussion about physical contact with others.

Materials: An open area in which to form a circle.

Time: Approximately 15 minutes.

Directions: Participants form a circle. Everyone extends the right palm. Then instruct everyone to put the left index finger on the palm of the person on the left. When you give the signal to start, each person tries to "get" or trap the finger of the neighbor at the same time trying not to be "gotten." After trying this a few times for the right-hand-dominant folks' having an advantage, switch hands. After a time, initiate a discussion on the appropriateness of physical touch, from handshakes to hugs, high-fives to back slaps, etc. This is an area where much uncertainty exists, and an open discussion is very much in order.

15. Airborne [S]

Purpose:
To provide a fun and engaging activity and build esprit de corps, with low-level challenge.

Materials:
A bunch of balloons and a hazard-free area.

Time:
Variable, 10–20 minutes.

Directions:
Divide the group into trios. Each small group joins hands and is given a balloon that it must keep in the air for the designated time period. Members may use any part of their body to keep the balloon aloft, but they must also keep their hands clasped the entire time. Then to put some challenge into the game, the leader calls out a body part, such as "elbow," and that becomes the only part participants can use for keeping their balloons airborne. Call out a different body part about every 15–20 seconds. A sequence of body parts such as "hand and foot" can be called out. For a real test, the direction of "no body parts" can be called to see how the trios solve that problem.

At some point change the composition of the triads, with one person moving to the right. If you do that a second time, everyone will have been in a group with everyone else.

Discussion following this activity gives students an opportunity to reflect on the experience and what they learned.

16. Back-To-Back ▪

Purpose: To demonstrate that success requires the support of others.

Materials: No special materials needed, but participants should have appropriate clothing.

Time: 15 minutes and up.

Directions: Participants when paired off stand back-to-back with their elbows interlocked. Using each other's back for support, the partners must try to sit on the floor and stretch out their legs. Then, while keeping their elbows locked, the partners must try to stand up without slipping or falling down. You may purposefully put together pairs of uneven height or weight, depending on your sensitivity to the degree the group has already become a "family."

You may also at some point let volunteers try to perform the exercise in record time. Discussion afterwards can point out what made the task easy or difficult.

17. Puppet on a String ◙

Purpose: To demonstrate the importance—and difficulty— of teamwork.

Materials: No equipment required.

Time: 20 minutes.

Directions: In this activity the leader is the puppet master, and the entire group acts as the puppet. This game works best with a large group. The whole group forms a circle and then arranges itself to make up a stick figure (puppet), i.e. a small circle of participants for the head, a short line for the neck, a longer line of participants for body, two arms, and two legs. After they're assembled, the leader (puppet master) gives a series of directions, one at a time, and participants must act as a group and perform the actions, such as

1) Your head is itchy, scratch it!

2) There's a soccer ball at your feet, kick it!

3) Your shoe is untied, tie it!

4) Your nose is running, blow it!

5) You dropped something, bend down and pick it up! This usually elicits laughter and many comments.

Participants can become the puppet master and suggest movements.

18. Obstacle Course ◉

Purpose:
To improve participants' ability to listen and follow directions—while getting some exercise.

Materials:
Use hula hoops, balls, jump ropes, or other materials you have available. A gym will make a good course, but an open area or even outside can work. It could take a few minutes to set up the equipment, and you should have the directions written out.

Time:
20–35 minutes.

Directions:
Set up materials in different parts of the gym—jump ropes in one corner, a straight line made with masking tape down the middle of the gym, hula hoops in another corner, a basketball by a goal, or some other item in another corner. Start by informing participants you will call out the directions only once, and you will say them all at once so they will have to listen and remember. Then call out the directions clearly and slowly. Possible directions would be: "Run to the hula hoops. Use the hoop to 'hula,' making five clockwise hoops and four counterclockwise hoops. Hop on your right foot to the top of the line, then hop on your left foot down the line. Walk backwards to the jump rope area. Jump five times with both feet and four times alternating feet."

Limit the directions to a reasonable number of steps for a first round, Then consider a second round with different directions. To ensure the directions are followed correctly, identify a few referees. The activity can be done in pairs as well as by individuals.

19. Just for Fun ▲

Purpose: To laugh!

Materials: None. This activity can be completed in a classroom. A
                timekeeper is needed.

Time: 10 minutes plus.

Directions: Participants forming two equal lines face one another and are
                labeled with the school colors, such as greens and golds. One
                color is designated to go first. All the members of that team try
                for 30 seconds to make those on the other team laugh. Those
                found laughing sometime during the 30 seconds are then
                recruited to the other side. Then the sides are reversed for a
                30-second turn. Four turns constitutes a game. The side ending
                with the most members after four turns wins.

                Some may offer to keep a straight face longer. Let them
                try—maybe a "face-off" to determine King or Queen Straight
                Face.

20. Picture Me Positively ▉ ▉

Purpose: To build students' self-concepts and enhance the total
               group's sense of worth.

Materials: Paper, colored pencils, markers, or paint. Tape is needed to
               display pictures, and several mirrors should be available to
               students.

Time: 50–60 minutes.

Directions: Each participant quietly draws a self-portrait as skillfully and
               detailed as possible. When a student is satisfied with his or her
               representation, he or she signs the picture and puts it on the
               wall, still with no talking. Students begin to circulate throughout
               the room to view the portraits. Then they draw the names
               of two or three others of their group and write a positive
               statement about those persons on their portrait. Don't rush this
               activity. Let everyone enjoy quiet time viewing the portraits,
               reflecting on the individuals, and considering the positive
               characteristics of one another.

21. Desperate Measures ⬛L ⬛S

Purpose: To learn about measurement units based on the body and be active.

Materials: None required, although you as leader should have some background information at hand.

Time: 50 plus minutes.

Directions: Depending on the time available, have participants work alone or with partners, with the same scale (body size, room size, campus size) and dimension (linear, volume); assign them to one of a range, or have them rotate through in centers. For linear body measurements have participants estimate how many wrists would equal a neck or head. For the room measurement, students can use feet, elbow-to-fingertip (cubits), or body lengths as the unit; for the campus, they can use the length of several students laid down end-to-end. They can also come up with a name for this unit. For any of these linear measurements they can use a length of string to determine the accuracy of their estimations. They can also determine if in general there is any standard foot or elbow-to-fingertip (cubit) length. For volume measurements, participants can determine the group's standard "pinch" by averaging how many cupcake sprinkles students can pick up in one "pinch"; they can determine the group's standard "handful" by averaging the number of marbles students can pick up in one hand. This activity provides data for students to practice graphing, comparative writing, and the concepts of range, mean, and average.

22. Muralize ⬛ ⬛

Purpose: To provide students an opportunity to express themselves creatively.

Materials: Very large sheets of blank paper (the larger the better), markers, paint, and paintbrushes.

Time: This activity can be completed at one time but is best done at various times over a long period. It need not be done as a large group and can be featured on the classroom wall.

Directions: Place the very large sheet of blank paper on a wall. To start the mural, write a thought-provoking phrase such as "It's tough being a kid because..." Then individuals complete that phrase with a few words and an illustration. Other starters could be value words such as "mutual respect" or "responsibility," or a local or national issue in the news.

23. Taking a Stand ⬛L⬛S

Purpose: To help students become more knowledgeable about adolescent health concerns and issues in an informal setting.

Materials: Signs to label each corner of the room with *strongly agree, agree, disagree,* and *strongly disagree* and a list of provocative statements related to adolescent health and fitness are needed.

Time: 30 minutes.

Directions: After a moment to reflect on the statement read, students go to the corner that represents their positions or beliefs. Then some in each corner will be asked to elaborate on the reason for their position. This prompts discussion that may lead some to switch positions, a most acceptable practice. Statements to get the activity started include

- Sports is a socially sanctioned form of violence.

- Refusing to fight takes more courage than fighting.

- We don't have to be concerned about boys' developing eating disorders, only girls.

- There are health disparities among the races.

- It is human nature to fight.

- Homework (or TV, or various video games) is a reason students are less physically active than they should be.

- Cyberbullying is a form of violence.

- Being sedentary is dangerous to your health.

- People are genetically programmed to have certain health problems; there is nothing you can do about it.

This activity can be used at the beginning of a unit and then repeated using some new, more specific questions at the end of the unit. Discussion reveals changes in understandings and attitudes.

24. Nutrition Investigation ⬛

Purpose: To lead students in considering healthy lifestyles and engage them in creating skits.

Materials: Health terms printed on small pieces of paper and placed in a hat or bag (terms represent a nutrient—carbohydrate, protein, fat, vitamins, and minerals—or another factor in a healthy lifestyle such as exercise, good nutrition, moderation, periodic medical assessment), books and Internet access for information gathering, areas for small groups to practice scenarios away from others.

Time: 45 minutes or more. May be done over two sessions.

Directions: Place students in small groups of 3–5. Groups select a term from the bag and have 15 or more minutes to investigate the term using resources available and understand its importance to good health. Then each group collaborates in creating and performing a skit that demonstrates the role of its term in promoting healthy living.

Cognitive Development

Problem solving, decision making, creativity, brain puzzles

These activities offer students supported, stimulating opportunities to engage in complex and creative kinds of thinking. They could be used any time as independent activities, or perhaps at the start of a major unit. Many will lead to subsequent studies or student-generated investigations.

Group problem solving is best when there is not a single solution and when communication is involved (see also related activities in Section Three). Students should come to realize that initial ideas are not always best, generating alternatives is a useful skill, and the sum of a group's work can be greater than the sum of its individual members' work (synergy). Given the cognitive development of most adolescents, this point is easily overlooked.

Legend: **T** activities with a thinking focus

LS activities that develop listening skills

C activities that address higher level thinking development and more creativity

1. Recollection ▪️

Purpose: To demonstrate the point that note taking and teamwork increase one's ability to remember more.

Materials: Gather 50 miscellaneous small items such as a ball, fingernail file, hat, mirror, key, toy, photo, candle, pen, orange, book, etc. You'll also need a tray and a cloth to cover the tray.

Time: 25 minutes.

Directions: Put half of the items on the tray and cover them with the cloth. Tell participants that you are going to show them a tray of miscellaneous items, and they should try to remember as many items as they can. Display the tray with 25 items for 60 seconds, then cover the tray. Talk to the group about most anything for a minute. Then have participants write down as many items as they can remember. Uncover the items on the tray and let the participants determine how many correct items they had remembered.

Do the activity again, displaying a new set of 25 items for just 30 seconds, but allow participants to take notes. Ask each participant to count the number of items listed, then organize the group into teams of four and have them combine their lists. Reveal the new items on the tray and determine first how many correct items individual participants remembered and then the number the teams listed after the 30-second viewing. Draw conclusions about the difference in outcome between the two situations. If necessary, point out to participants their ability to write more items in half the time (30 seconds) than when they had 60 seconds as well as the fact that teams were able to list more items than individuals. Conclude the activity by asking participants how they would apply the principles of note taking and working in teams to other situations that require memorizing and recollecting.

2. What Else? Ⓒ

Purpose: To promote creativity and rationality. This activity can be
              tailored for a number of different situations.

Materials: An intriguing picture from a magazine or the Internet, such as
              an old woman pulling a shiny wagon of fruit.

Time: 25 minutes.

Directions: Display the picture briefly then ask each person to write down
              in one minute, what he or she thinks is going on in the picture.
              Then point out some details—e.g., the fruits are tropical, the
              wagon is overloaded, the road is newly paved—and ask all
              participants to expand their individual lists with alternative
              explanations for another minute by saying "What else could it
              be?" Explanations from this picture might be, "She is addicted
              to fruit and has to have it with her at all times; The woman is
              taking the fruit to her grandchildren in the city; She won the
              wagon in town while she was buying fruit and is going home."
              or "She lost her grocery bag and borrowed a wagon from the
              neighbors to haul groceries."

              Then, leaving the picture up for viewing, tell students to
              physically move and find a partner, share lists, and add
              to them if they so desire. Remove the picture and instruct
              partners to identify from their lists the best explanation for
              the action the picture captured and provide a rationale
              for their choice. These would be shared with the large
              group and, by consensus, the group would select the best
              explanation. Finally, display the picture again and scour for
              details, helping the group determine if it had made the "right"
              choice. Then discuss the meaning of "good reasoning" and
              why some explanations make better sense than others. This
              helps students learn that not all reasons are equally valid and
              persuasive, and the process can be used to help identify the
              better explanation for an event.

3. Truth or Consequences ▪

Purpose: To consider appropriate school behaviors and the relationship between behavior and consequence.

Materials: Copies of the worksheet "Can You Identify Behavior?" for each student.

Time: Approximately two 25-minute sessions.

Directions: Discuss the dictionary definitions of *behavior* and *consequences* and review the difference between positive and negative consequences. After the review, distribute the worksheet to be used to assess understanding. Read each situation aloud to the whole group, discussing the behavior consequences and whether the consequences are positive or negative. Then introduce the term *control*, eliciting a definition from the group. Finally review the stories, asking students to tell whether or not the person could control the consequences. Ask for volunteers to share their examples on the back of the worksheet. You can also have students respond orally or in writing to the following application questions:

- How much control do you have over the consequences of what you do at school?

- How does it make you feel to know that you can or cannot control the consequences?

Can You Identify Behavior?

In each of the boxed situations below, identify the behaviors with B, the consequences with C, and indicate if the consequences are positive (+) or negative (-).

1.

> Maia is daydreaming in class. When the teacher calls on her, she does not know the answer—or even the question.

2.

> Carlos leans on a lamppost. All the lights in the city go out.

3.

> John's friends ask him to play ball after school. John turns them down in order to complete a project due in social studies the next day, which will keep his grade of A intact.

4.

> You had a fight with your best friend. You stay out in the hall to get it settled, and as a result, you're late for class.

5.

> Someone calls you a name on the playground. You walk away, and everyone there calls you "chicken."

6.

> Andy is in the boys' room. A friend is smoking in there and wants him to share the cigarette. Andy says, "No," but his friend says, "Aw, come on . . . " Andy stays, smokes, and is late to class.

On the back of this sheet, write an example of your own that tells about one of your behaviors and the consequences.

4. Investigate Decision-Making Processes ▪

Purpose: To learn about the decision-making process and apply it.

Materials: Use the following page, "Steps in Decision Making," as a
                model for the activity.

Time: 20 minutes.

Directions: This activity begins with a brief presentation of a decision and
                ends with each person, pair, or small group applying the steps
                of the process to a decision it makes. The particular model you
                follow is less important than applying it to a personal decision.
                You can use it frequently until students learn how and why to
                apply without prompting. On the following page is a model
                and one example a pair of students in an advisory group
                completed.

                You should use this activity more than once.

Steps in Decision Making

1. Define the goal (Shelly wants to be happy).

2. Identify the alternatives. (Shelly can spend the night at Shauna's house on a school night or study for exam, but she knows she can't do both)

3. Analyze alternatives. (Spending the night will be fun. Shauna and Shelly will become better friends. Studying will not be fun tonight, but Shelly should do much better on the exam by studying. If she does better, then she gets a better grade; maybe she could go to college, which would make herself and her parents happy.)

4. Rank alternatives. (This is hard. But the second one seems the better thing to do, so we rank it No. 1.)

5. Judge the highest-ranked alternatives. (Studying is better because it will make three people happy—Shelly and her parents; but it will take a long time to know if it were the right thing to do. College is years away, and she can't tell if she will get in because of one grade.)

6. Implement "best" alternative and see if you reach your goal. (She studied and made a 91 on the test, which she probably wouldn't if she hadn't studied. She missed Shauna, but she is happy with her grade and so are her parents. It was a good decision. She is going to Shauna's this weekend.)

In this case Shelly's example shows the group how a sign of maturity is being able to delay gratification and that Shelly's reasoning showed that she was making important strides toward adulthood.

5. May I Have Your Attention Please? ⬛ ⬛

Purpose: To teach the skill of hypothesis testing, a process widely used to solve scientific and other problems.

Materials: Use photocopies of this folktale about a Talmudic scholar, which illustrates four steps: 1) identify the problem, 2) propose a hypothesis, 3) test the hypothesis, and 4) draw a conclusion.

Time: 20 minutes or more.

Directions: Each student, after reading the folktale should place a "P" next to any line where a problem is being suggested or a question asked; an "H" next to lines that contain the best tentative explanation (hypothesis) that would solve the problem; a "T" to identify those sections where data is used to test an hypothesis; and finally a "C" next to lines where conclusions are being stated.

In order to help develop students' metacognition about problem solving, the group should discuss the steps of the process each identified. When discussing the student results it should be noted that the woman broke her problem into manageable sub-problems and used the data at her disposal. Then students should begin to use the process identified in the story of breaking problems into convenient "chunks" to work on and to systematically gather and apply data to help guide problem-solving efforts generally. The group, probably in small teams, should try to write similar folktales that call on the power of observation and hypothesis testing to help further develop metacognitive skills. In doing this, the steps will become clear, and the whole process will be understood more fully.

A Folktale

An older woman, who had spent the last several years in the United States, was returning to her village in South Africa for a much-needed visit. After flying to Johannesburg, she purchased a bus ticket to take her the rest of the way to her community. While standing in line to buy her ticket she noticed an exceedingly well-dressed man in front of her buying a ticket to the same poor village. Deciding that it would not be polite to ask the man his business in the village, she spent her time on the bus, seated across from him in an ideal spot for observation, trying to discern his reason for visiting her rural town.

She noticed the man was reading a novel in her native language, in which few books are written, and guessed that he might be going to the annual village festival to celebrate the harvest. Many people came to the village at that time. "But no," she said to herself. "The festival is more than a month out, and no man dressed and educated such as he would wait around for a festival."

Next she posited that the man was going to find himself a wife skilled in the ways of her village to take with him back to his home. But on closer observation she saw that the man wore a wedding ring on his left hand, and she said to herself, "That certainly can't be it. He's not of a marriageable age either."

Looking over the monogrammed briefcase he carried, the woman wondered if the man might be a lawyer. She had heard from her cousin that her village was going to sue the state for water rights. He was dressed in a distinguished fashion as attorneys in the United States often are. But when he snapped open his briefcase she saw no computer, no documents, just a number of books.

"Books?" she asked herself, "Who uses books?" It was then that she decided the man was a teacher. Given his age and his bearing she decided that he had also had a number of years of experience as a teacher. Then remembering the difficulty of the titles of the books she had seen in his case, she was led to believe he was a college professor. If he was a professor he no doubt had earned a Ph.D. and should be addressed as "Doctor." He must be going to her village to recruit students for the new college that was rumored to be opening in the district the next year!

Eager to start a conversation with her companion and to see if she were correct, the woman took another peek at the monogrammed bag with the bold "S" on it. "Dr. Smith, would you mind opening a window? It's a bit stuffy in here."

Startled, the man replied, "I don't mind at all. But how did you know I am Dr. Smith?" "Oh it was quite apparent" replied the satisfied woman.

6. Creativity—An Essential Skill c

Purpose: To practice creativity.

Materials: A copy of "Components of Creativity" for each participant.

Time: To talk through the handout may take about 20 minutes, while
              the problem-solving portion can take from 10–30 minutes
              depending on the problem.

Directions: Distribute the handout "Components of Creativity" and review
              it with the participants. Have students suggest examples or
              ideas. Then have them suggest possible "fun" problems, some
              from school, that they might encounter. Choose two or three
              to practice on.

Components of Creativity

Creativity, some believe, consists of four components 1) fluency, 2) flexibility, 3) elaboration, and 4) originality.

Fluency in writing refers to having many ideas that can be promoted by phrases such as

- Think of as many as possible...
- Brainstorm a list...
- Generate alternatives for...
- Note all of the situations in which...

Flexibility refers to change, so helpful words are

- Substitute _____ for _____ ...
- Modify/adapt...
- Rearrange/reverse...
- Speculate what might happen if...
- Eliminate...
- Put _____ and _____ together...

Elaboration calls for adding, so think

- Build on to that...
- Extend your thinking to...
- Make it more _____ by adding...
- Expand the idea by including...

Originality means difference, so try

- Create a new way to...
- What is the wildest way you could...?
- What is an unusual method for...?
- Show your own ideas for...
- Imagine how you would...
- Go out on a limb and suggest...

7. Swift Sphere ∎

Purpose: To engage in some problem-solving strategies that involve cooperation by the group.

Materials: No equipment, although a sufficient open space is needed for the group to form a circle.

Time: 15 minutes or more.

Directions: The group forms a circle (sphere) with you included. You direct the people in the group to toss the ball across the circle (not next to a tosser) to each person once and only once until the ball comes back to you as speedily as possible. The first time through, instruct participants to put their hands in front of them until they've been tossed the ball and then they should keep their hands at their sides. For the second time through, follow the same order but have someone time the sequence. Then challenge the group to set a time goal and work together to meet the goal. Each person should touch the ball in the order originally established. Allow some time for brainstorming and trying several suggestions. If the goal is reached, designate the group a "swift sphere." Depending on how readily the group takes on the challenge to complete the tossing quickly, this activity can go on for some time.

8. Blockbusters LS

Purpose: To improve listening skills and promote academic success. This activity came from Chris Elvin at http://www.eflclub.com/elvin/publications/highmotivationlistening.html but was first introduced as a quiz game show in Britain about 30 years ago. Using a five by five grid as shown allows for greater coverage of vocabulary, but you can use a four by four grid as in the original.

Materials: A transparency copy of the grid.

Time: 10–25 minutes.

Directions: Make a transparency copy of the grid and write a different letter of the alphabet in each hexagon. Divide participants into two teams and pick a student to choose a letter. From a previously prepared word list such as vocabulary words the students encounter for a unit or "power builders," choose a word whose first letter matches the student's choice and explain this word to your class. The first team to guess the word correctly claims the hexagon and chooses to continue either vertically or horizontally. After that selection is established the alternate team must make its moves in the opposite direction. To win the game, a team must connect all the way from top to bottom, or from side to side.

9. Newspaper Tower ∎

Purpose: To engage everyone in a creative problem-solving activity; to build the tallest tower using only two sheets of newspaper.

Materials: Two full sheets of newspaper for each team of two or three—with lots of additional newspaper available—and a ruler.

Time: 30 minutes or more depending on discussion, if a second round is carried out, or if tape is used.

Directions: The challenge is to build the tallest tower, using only two sheets of newspaper, without using tape, staples, glue, or other materials. The paper can be bent, folded, or torn. Each team should plan a design and keep redesigning it until it can't go any higher. When teams are finished building, measure the height of the towers. The total group should discuss designs that did and did not work. The group members can also discuss (and try) how they would change the design if given 20 cm. of tape. They will likely want to make a second effort, with new sheets, based on their experiences.

10. Logic Puzzles ▣ ▣

Purpose: To engage everyone in activities that call for a creative use of logic and critical thinking.

Materials: Four puzzles.

Time: 15–45 minutes.

Directions: There are many ways to use these puzzles. Four small groups could each work on one of the puzzles then exchange them, or all groups could work on the same puzzle at the same time to see which group solves the puzzle first. Each of the puzzles could be used as a quick, independent activity. There are still many other ways to use them as will occur to you when you study them. Discussion should accompany their use. You or the students may find other puzzles in magazines or on the Internet. Often a student will offer to create a puzzle for the group to solve on a later occasion.

Passing a Note

Jack has a major crush on Jill. During study hall, he finally gathers all of his courage and writes her a note asking her to the school dance on Saturday night. The note passes to five students (who all read it) before it gets to Jill. Just as Jill gets the note, Ms. Wilson, the teacher, confiscates it. After reading the note, she wants to know all who were involved in the note-passing incident. She questions the students, and gets the following responses.

The girl studying English passed it to Deondre who passed it to the girl in green. Josefina passed it to the boy in blue, who gave it to Alexis who was reading.

The girl in red gave it to Jill.
Jack first gave it to Maia who was studying English.
The girl in red who was reading got the note from Derrick.
Ms. Wilson remembers the following facts from study hall:
- Deondre was wearing yellow.
- Derrick was studying French.
- The girl in green was studying science.

From the information given by the students, can you determine what color each culprit was wearing, the subject he or she was studying, and the order that he or she received the note? Use the chart below to help you.

	Eng	Fre	Rdg	Sci	Mat	Red	Grn	Blu	B;a	Yel	1st	2nd	3rd	4th	5th
Maia															
Deondre															
Alexis															
Josefina															
Derrick															
1st															
2nd															
3rd															
4th															
5th															
Red															
Grn															
Blu															
Bla															
Yel															

Who Threw the Spit Ball?

It was the last class of the afternoon, and Mr. Anleyt was reading from a book as the seventh grade algebra class finished its homework. Engrossed in his reading, he had his nose buried in the book. All of a sudden from the right side of the room, a big, well-constructed spitball flashed past his head and smacked against the whiteboard behind him. Glancing up startled, he could tell only that it had come from the row closest to the window or the row immediately inside of that. Also from the angle, it appeared to come from the front half of one of those rows. All the students from that side of the room were seemingly intent on their work, and no one was looking up. From the other side of the room, however, it was a different story. Several students were looking around with a grin on their faces as if they had seen the whole thing. But of course, no one would admit to anything. So Mr. Anleyt was left to discover the culprit himself. He narrowed the field of possible delinquents to four students and began to question them. He asked the question, "Who threw that spitball?" Each of the four students made one statement.

MARIA: I didn't do it.

JACKSON: I didn't do it.

MARKUS: Abramson did it.

LU: Markus is telling the truth.

Being a very clever teacher, Mr. Anleyt knew that only two students were telling the truth. So he questioned them again. He asked, "Who threw that spitball?" Again each student made one statement.

MARIA   Lu did it.

ANNIE: Maria is lying.

MARTIN: Annie didn't do it.

JACKSON: Martin didn't do it.

"Now this is interesting," thought Mr. Anleyt, "Each student who lied before has told the truth, and each one who told the truth now lied! Oh well, no matter, I know who the culprit is!"

DO YOU? You may need this chart to help solve the puzzle!

NAMES	Jackson	Martin	Lu	Abramson
Maria				
John				
Markus				
Annie				

Occupations Puzzle

Each of three friends is engaged in a different occupation. By a strange coincidence their names, Ms. Carpenter, Mr. Mason, and Ms. Painter, are the same as their trades, but not necessarily respectively.

The following statements were made about the three friends but it turned out that only one statement was true. Who is what?

- Ms. Carpenter is not a painter.

- Mr. Mason is not a carpenter.

- Ms. Carpenter is a carpenter.

- Mr. Mason is not a painter.

Play on Words

Use the shape or the placement of the words to help you decipher the meaning of a popular phrase:

big big	search
ignore ignore	search
MEREPEAT	go it it it it
faredce	lang4uage
gesg	Give Get
segg	Give Get
gegs	Give Get
gges	Give Get
ssssssssssc	XQQME
insult + injury	13579 AZ
you cont ol r	AALLLL
bad bad	to rn
BB	Must get here
AA	Must get here
RR	Must get here
Hlicd	fa th

Answers

Passing a Note

First-Maia-red, studying English
Second-Jarvis-yellow, studying math
Third-Josefina-green, studying science
Fourth-Derrick-blue, studying French
Fifth-Alexis-black, reading

Who Threw the Spit Ball?

Markus Martin threw the spit ball

Occupations Puzzler

Either the first or the fourth statements must be true, because they both can't be false. If both were false, then both people would be painters (there must be three different occupations). Therefore either Ms. Carpenter or Mr. Mason is the painter. The second and third statements must be false. The falsity of the second statement makes Mr. Mason the carpenter and establishes Ms. Carpenter as the painter. Ms. Painter must be the mason.

Play on Words

1) Too big to ignore

2) Search high and low

3) Repeat after me

4) Go for it

5) Red in the face

6) Foreign language

7) Scrambled eggs

8) Forgive and forget

9) Tennessee

10) Excuse me

11) Adding insult to injury

12) Odds and ends

13) You are out of control

14) All in all

15) Too bad

16) Torn apart

17) Parallel bars

18) Three Musketeers

19) Mixed up child

20) Blind fate

11. Ten Measurements ∎

Purpose: To help participants develop a better conceptual
              understanding of measurement.

Materials: Ten measurement activities.

Time: 25 minutes or more, depending on how it is organized.

Directions: As with some other activities, all participants can work on the
              same task, or the tasks can be distributed or rotated among
              members of the group. Give students a handout sheet with
              the following instructions or ones you develop:

Make up your own measuring system using whatever you would like as a basic
unit—a book, a rope, a scarf, etc., and figure out the following measurements:

1. What is the combined height of all the members of the group?

2. Who has the longest hair? How long is it?

3. Put all your left feet in a line and measure them.

4. Who has the longest ears?

5. Make a circle, as big as you can, by joining hands. What is the diameter
    of the circle? the perimeter?

6. How long are all of our arms?

7. Who has the longest arms?

8. Measure our little fingers. How long are they when all are combined?

9. Who has the largest head?

10. Convert measurements among units. For instance 1 comb = ___ belt

More variations are possible, including establishing a second unit that is
related to the first, as in inches and feet. You might want to follow this activity
with the measurement of time and introduce Roman numbers.

12. Pass the Basket L

Purpose:
To develop listening, communicating, and sharing skills, and to build trust within the group.

Materials:
Chairs should be placed in a circle so all can see one another. Prepare a list of memory-stimulating questions or phrases. Put each one on a strip of paper, fold the strips, and place them in a basket. You can make the questions or prompts specific to certain goals you have for the group (such as talking about different cultures) or this can be more of an icebreaker-type activity with general questions.

Time:
25–45 minutes, depending on size of group.

Directions:
One person selects a prompt from the basket and in about one to two minutes shares his or her response to the question. After telling his or her story, this person passes the basket on to the next one in the circle.

Suggested prompts include: favorite memory of mom; favorite book, song, or movie, and why; favorite season and favorite thing to do in that season; funniest best friend story. Questions could include: Who have you been closest to as you were growing up? Has that person changed now that you are an adolescent? What roles do you hope to fill as an adult? What are you able to do better than anyone you know? If you were a dog, what breed would you be and why? How did you get your name?

Other individuals may offer comments or share a similar story. Don't rush this activity. At the end of the storytelling, see if anyone can name the topic or the essence of each person's story.

13. ABC ▣

Purpose: This old favorite from the days before TV develops concentration, memory, and creativity.

Materials: No equipment needed. Group members should sit in a circle so they can see one another.

Time: 15–20 minutes.

Directions: In this activity, one participant will start by stating the first name he or she has assumed for this game, the place he will visit, and what he will pack in his suitcase appropriate for a trip to the locale. These three (name, destination, and item) must begin with the letter "A." The second person will restate all that the first person identified and add her name, her destination, and the item in her suitcase, all beginning with the letter "B." The third person will restate fully what the first two said and add his information. This continues until the last person has made it all of the way through the alphabet. To make the game more difficult, the first person can have an "A" name, a "B" locale, and a "C" item, while the second person has a "B" name, a "C" locale, and a "D" item, etc.

14. What's the Difference? ▪

Purpose: To help students develop attention to details and comparison skills for intellectual development.

Materials: Collect "Which Two of the Pictures Are the Same?" panels from the Sunday comics and puzzle books found on magazine stands. Have enough for each participant to look at several. Students will need paper, pencils, and markers for the design process. (More technologically advanced teachers can complete this as a computer-enhanced activity, but I've only completed it "the old-fashioned way."

Time: Could take up to 60 minutes.

Directions: Distribute the samples and ask participants to pay attention to the kinds of changes that are the most subtle and difficult to spot. Then encourage each student to create his or her own set of five panels, which can then be shared with the rest of the group. After participants have worked with the puzzles, lead a discussion about the skills developed in the solution and creation of the look-alike panels.

15. Touch the Ball ∎

Purpose: To engage students in a collaboratively solved problem.

Materials: A variety of objects of various sizes, such as a soccer ball, a softball, a tennis ball, a golf ball, a tube of lip gloss, a large paper clip, and a dime—and an open area.

Directions: Ask the group to stand in a circle, facing inward. Place the largest object in the middle of the circle and tell the participants that they must all touch the object without touching each other. Let them talk it out and try out a plan— and then a better plan to do it more quickly. Once they figure out how to arrange themselves so that they can do this in 10 seconds, give them a smaller object. Work all the way down to the dime! Depending on the readiness of the group, you can add rules, such as all must touch the object in a certain amount of time or even simultaneously.

Note if someone assumed leadership and what was the result. Discuss with group.

16. Magic Wand C

Purpose: To promote discussion and engage in a problem-solving
             activity that helps participants learn about others' desires and
             frustrations.

Materials: A "magic" wand or decorated stick to simulate a wand.

Directions: Participants should sit in a circle so they can all see each
             other. The leader can participate in this activity. Tell the
             students the following: "You have just found a magic wand
             that allows you to change three school-related activities or
             conditions. You can change anything you want. How would
             you change yourself, your school, your teachers, classmates,
             an important project, or something else?"

             Give them a few minutes to jot down ideas before they share
             responses. Give the wand to one who indicated a readiness
             to speak. The speaker shares the changes that would benefit
             him or her or the school and passes the wand to another
             student.

             When individuals begin talking, have them provide a
             rationale for the changes proposed. After most have spoken,
             allow everyone to compare lists to see if there is something
             in common to which group members could apply their
             concerted efforts toward making a change. Another variation
             is to have them seriously and thoughtfully discuss what they
             would change if they become principal for a month. A plan to
             pursue some change as a group project may evolve.

17. Do My Eyes Deceive Me? ▣ ▣

Purpose: To have indoor fun and develop observation skills.

Materials: Copies of one model should be available for each student. One example of "Hidden Objects Pictures" can be found on the Internet at http://www.tappi.org/paperu/fun_games/hiddenPics_classroom.pdf, while an example of a puzzle where the differences must be spotted is located at http://www.astrohoroscopes.com/puzzles/spotthediff/spotthedifference_lion.html

Other starters can come from newspaper comics or magazines such as *Highlights*.

Time: Anywhere from 5 to 50 minutes.

Directions: Distribute a puzzle to each person. It can be a "hidden object picture" puzzle where students must find the items obscured within a picture of a larger scene, or a "spot the difference" puzzle of a comic strip. In each of four or five frames there is a drawing of a nearly identical scene with minor changes; the student must identify the subtle differences in all but two identical frames. A variation of this can be found in magazines where two nearly identical pictures are exhibited side by side, and the students must identify the several small differences between the two.

However, the more challenging part of this activity comes when students are instructed to create their own "hidden object picture" or puzzle of images to be compared. These might be done by volunteers on their own over several days and then presented as challenges to the group. Created puzzles can be photocopied and distributed. The group can analyze puzzles for their difficulty and even create a third round of puzzles based on strategies that make puzzles more difficult to solve.

18. Tesselations 🅣 🄲

Purpose: To identify patterns using mathematical thinking and create a tesselation.

Materials: None, other than whatever background information and directions you may want to share.

Time: Depending on how deeply you want to address the mathematical principles involved, this activity can take up to four hours to complete. However students can "play around" with shapes and patterns and create tessellations of geometric shapes in as few as 25 minutes. Discerning and creating a tessellating pattern of a real object á la M. C. Escher, a famous graphic artist, will take longer to complete.

Directions: Tessellations are repeating patterns on a plane with no overlapping or spaces between the shapes such as the simple tessellation of triangles found below. Tessellating patterns can be found in quilts and mosaic tiles.

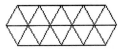

Encourage students to come up with and color their complex creations, which would then be displayed in the hall.

19. Analogy ▣

Purpose: To engage in analogical and metaphorical thinking

Materials: A whiteboard or other venue for brainstorming ideas as a
                whole group. Paper, pencil, or word processor will be needed
                for creating individual analogies.

Time: 20–30 minutes plus additional time if individuals create
                analogies.

Directions: Brainstorm a list of all of the classic analogies or metaphors
                that participants learn at school or on television. These include
                the brain as a computer, the cell as a factory, middle school
                as a jungle, school as prison, or life as a box of chocolates.
                Some humorous writing analogies can be found at http://
                writingenglish.wordpress.com/2006/09/12/the-25-funniest-
                analogies-collected-by-high-school-english-teachers/

                Review the relationship presented by the analogy. Discuss
                why and how the analogy "works." Also discuss how it "breaks
                down" or fails to be a perfect comparison. Finally, students
                can work in pairs or alone to create new analogies to share
                with the group.

20. So You Wanna Be a Brainiac? ■

Purpose: To learn about how the brain works and influences aspects of learning and to lead to students' becoming more self-regulated and metacognitive learners.

Materials: Copies of "Brain and Learning Facts" handouts to be distributed to each participant.

Time: 20 minutes—but activity will likely lead to more time later.

Directions: Participants can read the handout Brain and Learning Facts and discuss its content. Then, individuals or pairs can conduct more comprehensive investigations on the Internet of such topics as "creativity," "multiple intelligences," "learning styles," or "metacognition." Later, they can present this information to the whole group and use what they have learned to help them set goals toward becoming more self-regulated learners. Some pretty heavy discussions should result and have real long-term importance as students become more knowledgeable about the brain and learning, thereby becoming more sensitive to the strategies employed by teachers and moving toward becoming lifelong learners.

Brain and Learning Facts

What is learning?

Learning seems to take place in the brain and results in your being able to do something that you couldn't do before. When you "learn" your multiplication facts, you are able to use them to solve math problems. When you "learn" to recite the Gettysburg Address you are able to say it, when you couldn't do that before. If you "learn" to bake, and cakes and cookies appear at the end of a process, then you learned how to do something you weren't able to accomplish in the past. Learning takes place because the brain is organizing information in different ways that allow you to respond differently than you did in the past.

What is the brain? What does it have to do with learning?

The brain is one of many organs in the body, but it is the one that is the center of the nervous system. The brain is both "the mind" where thinking occurs as well as the part of the body that generates and controls behavior. It is the brain that is responsible for taking information from the environment and determining how to respond to it. Change in the different ways that the brain takes in information, organizes it, and tells the body how to respond is called "learning." People have preferences about how they learn best. They also tend to process information more on one side of the brain or the other. The brain is the source of creativity as well as the source of logical thought.

What does each half of the brain do?

The human brain consists of many components but is mainly divided into "halves." The left side processes information logically and seems to be in charge of understanding numbers and language. The right side is known as the more creative half of the brain and processes information as a "big picture." Of course no one uses only one side of the brain exclusively, so to make the most of your brainpower, you need to develop both halves. But be careful—most people tend to get into a rut and rely on one side more than the other, failing to take full advantage of this most marvelous organ.

How can I develop my creativity?

Human beings are creatures of habit. This is because habit is efficient. A habit is just a routine or a pattern of doing things. The brain is so efficient because in every experience—from reading a book, to talking with friends, to riding a bicycle—the two halves and the other components of our brains are processing the information and looking for patterns. When our mind recognizes a pattern, it makes a connection to things it already "knows" and then "stores" the experiences as part of a larger pattern. That is memory.

As the patterns are recognized by our brains, they become more strongly established, and our brains get into ruts.

A "rut" is the opposite of "creativity"; so creative people, people who develop both halves of their brains, tend to shake things up. They deliberately try to take a different view of things. Creative people don't let themselves fall into ruts. To release your creativity, you have to unlearn much of what you suspect is the "right" way to do things. So to "unlearn," try to do things the "wrong" way—read the book beginning with the last chapter, "talk" to your friends without making a sound, ride your bike with no hands! Always challenge yourself to avoid the ruts.

What can I do with this information?
As people mature they become better at using brain power. One thing you can do with this information is to practice being a better controller—of your impulses, of your study habits, of making the environment the best for your learning. You can also investigate a topic further such as "multiple intelligences" or "learning styles" and share the information with your teammates. Then decide on one thing you can do to improve your learning.

21. W-R-I-T—"We R It" Community Radio ▪

Purpose: To take responsibility for addressing community problems.

Materials
and time: Each project will vary in time and materials necessary.

Directions: This activity should begin with a real problem that is classroom
                related, such as deciding the "fair" way of deciding who
                can participate in field trips or ways to ensure students get to
                class on time. After students brainstorm and decide upon one
                solution, which is enacted and monitored, students are urged
                to look beyond the classroom for similar community problems.
                Following the model used for classroom-related solutions and
                depending on the complexity of the problem, students work in
                pairs or with the entire group to investigate and pose solutions
                for community challenges such as picking up roadside litter.
                Students should present solutions to appropriate community
                groups. This is a valuable extension of civic engagement
                that will help students transfer understanding of community
                maintenance from the smaller to the larger scale.

SECTION THREE

Social and Emotional Development

Communication and behaving responsibly toward others and self

To assist young adolescents in becoming responsible members of a group is a universally accepted goal of middle level education. Activities in this section will help students improve upon their inter- and intrapersonal awareness and practice communication, organizational, and leadership skills that will also further their academic success and self-esteem. These activities will provide problem-based learning experiences that will help students form a community from diverse individuals and become involved in society as members of democratic citizenry.

Communication is at the heart of being human. One important aspect of communication that needs to be learned is listening to others as a social skill not a cognitive skill. Many middle schoolers confuse listening with hearing. The activities here will strengthen listening skills to improve social and civic engagement and learning.

Legend: **G** activities that primarily promote group development

I activities that emphasize individual development

T activities that emphasize trust development

1. Have You Ever? ⓖ

Purpose: To help a group become better acquainted and find new connections among members.

Materials: This can be performed in the classroom by simply designating an area of the room to be the "yes" corral.

Time: 25 minutes.

Directions: Members gather together in a part of the room. When a question is asked, anyone who can answer "yes" goes to a designated place in the room and shares the condition or event. After this sharing, members return to the circle. After several examples are conducted, participants may suggest a question. Below are some "Have you ever" questions to get you started. The ones toward the end are more sensitive and should be attempted only when you believe there is a sufficient trust level to support such disclosures.

- Broken a bone? (Which one? When?)
- Taken a hot air balloon ride? (What was it like?)
- Been out of your time zone? (Where were you?)
- Won a monetary prize? (How much?)
- Been in a parade? (What for?)
- Met a famous person? (Who was it?)
- Ridden a double-decker bus? (Where was it?)
- Gotten lost on a hike? (How long were you lost?)
- "Regifted" a present? (What was it?)
- Eaten dessert before the meal? (What was the dessert?)
- Had a crush on a movie star? (Who was it?)
- Stayed up for over 24 hours? (What was going on?)
- Cried in front of others?
- Been embarrassed by your own behavior?
- Been the last player picked for a team game?
- Had a rumor started about you?
- Acted like you were listening when you weren't?
- Told a lie to get out of trouble?
- Cheated on an assignment?
- Let someone else take the blame when you were at fault?

2. Designing a Coat of Arms G

Purpose: To build group identity by developing a personalized coat of arms for the group.

Materials: Poster paper, felt pens, masking tape, scissors, rulers, etc.

Time: 40–50 minutes. Will likely require additional time on another day to complete.

Directions: Prior to the start of this session, the leader should outline a coat of arms on a very large sheet of chart paper, dividing it into six roughly equal parts. Cut the coat of arms into six sections, marking the top of each section on the back. Then divide the total group into six task groups. Ask each group to choose a facilitator and send that person to you. Explain to the facilitators that each group has a task to complete that will contribute to a total class project when put together. Randomly hand out one of the tasks on the following page to each facilitator. Point out the time constraints, answer any questions, and give each facilitator a section of the coat of arms. (Modify the tasks to make them appropriate to your group.) Monitor the groups, offering encouragement, clarification, and an occasional idea or suggestion as they work on their task. Make sure their drawings are placed right side up. When drawings are completed, each facilitator reads the group's task to the class and shows the results. Carefully attach the chart paper to another larger piece of paper to display the final product.

You probably should allow some settling time and come back to the coat of arms on another day. The "artists" probably will want to refine and improve their work, shifting the location of some sections to make it a more balanced piece and also coloring it differently. The total group will want to consider each group's ideas and possibly affirm or adapt the ideas, making the colors, symbols, etc., officially the standard.

If it turns out well, take a picture and make small prints for the group to use on agendas or book covers.

Tasks for Groups in Developing A Coat of Arms

Task for Group One

Decide on appropriate colors for the group and put them into a design on your part of the coat of arms. Be prepared to tell the class why you chose those colors. (Example: blue for loyalty, green for pride)

Task for Group Two

Decide on a mascot that could represent the group and then draw the mascot on your section of the coat of arms. Be prepared to tell why you chose the mascot. (Example: elephant, strong and intelligent)

Task for Group Three

Design a symbol that could represent the class and then draw the symbol on your section of the coat of arms. Be prepared to tell why you chose the symbol selected. (Example: four leaf clover, because you feel we are lucky to be in this group.)

Task for Group Four

Decide on a wish or ideal characteristic you would like to grant your whole school and then draw a symbol that represents the wish on your section of the coat of arms. Consider several before deciding on the "right" one. Be prepared to explain your wish and symbol to the class. (Example: our wish is for the winning attitude, and the symbol is a male and female with hands raised in victory.)

Task for Group Five

Decide on a motto for the group and put the motto on your section of the coat of arms. Be prepared to explain your choice to the class. (Examples: "United We Stand" is our motto, for it represents the way we should tackle problems this year.)

Task for Group Six

Decide on three words you hope people will remember this group for, and then write these words on your section of the coat of arms. Be prepared to explain your choice to the class. (Example: *caring, loyal,* and *strong,* because we think that these make good goals for our class.)

3. A Discussion About Noise 🄶

Purpose: To help students develop awareness of themselves and others.

Materials: Participants will need paper and pencil to record data, although data could be listed on a board for the entire group.

Time: Up to 60 minutes; may be done in two sessions.

Directions: Share with students the physical science definition for noise: "sound waves that are out of synchronization and work at cross purposes." Discuss noise as a metaphor for other phenomena. Then ask participants to talk with one or two others to identify the noisiest times of the day and the quietest times. Use these data gathered from the pairs or triads to determine whether the group has a consensus on the noisiest time. Continue to outline the things or conditions in class that make the most noise. Lastly, determine how noisy students would like class to be for various activities. Develop a symbol to represent the levels that can be used to help remind each other of appropriate volume levels. The book, *The Phantom Tollbooth** (1996), which is full of humorous and challenging word play, has an excellent reference to cacophony and dissonance and makes for a terrific read aloud.

*Justin, N. (1996). *The phantom tollbooth*. New York: Random House

4. Listen Carefully ▪

Purpose: To sharpen students' listening skills.

Materials: A sheet of paper and a pencil for each participant.

Time: 25 minutes.

Directions:

Start by informing the group that they are going to participate in an exercise to see how good they are at listening. Have them get their paper and pencils ready. Then say,

> "You need to listen carefully—no talking. Concentrate on your own paper and do your very best listening as you follow these instructions."
> 1. "Locate the upper left-hand corner of your paper."
>
> 2. "Now, move your pencil down the left-hand side of the page about two inches."
>
> 3. "From that point, move to the right two inches and make a dot."
>
> 4. "From that dot, draw a three-inch line to the right that is parallel with the top of the page."

At this point you may say: "Stop. In case you're feeling totally confused, I'm going to give you a chance to start over. Turn your papers over and I'll begin again. But no more second chances." (Read again all that is above and then continue through to the end without any more pauses.)

> 5. "Move back to the dot and draw a five-inch line parallel with the left-hand side of the paper and toward the bottom of your paper."
>
> 6. "From the bottom end of this line, go back up about three inches and draw another line three inches long to the right and parallel to the bottom of your paper."
>
> 7. "From the end of this line, draw a three-inch line down and parallel to the right-hand side of the paper."

8. "From the end of this line, go back up three inches and draw a two-inch line parallel to the right-hand side of the paper."

9. "Draw a vertical line from this point, joining with the right end of the first line you drew."

Now what have you drawn?

Let everyone see the individual results and discuss the reason why some letters weren't formed correctly. Point out that fact that one reason our minds tend to wander when we're trying to listen is the difference in the rate a person talks and the rate at which we can think. Normal speech is generally between 150–200 words per minute, while the mind is actually able to think at speeds up to a thousand words per minute. It takes a real effort to stay with a speaker.

If interest warrants, a more complicated letter or geometric figure might be attempted.

5. My Listening Skills ■

Purpose: To enable students to evaluate their own listening skills.

Materials: Each person in the group will need a copy of the handout
                "My Listening Skills Assessment."

Time: 30 plus minutes.

Directions: Distribute copies of the "My Listening Skills Assessment"
                handout to each member of the group. Ask students to review
                the list carefully and check any items they feel are generally
                true for them as individuals. In groups of two or three, have
                them compare their answers and discuss the where, when,
                and why they behaved in that way. They can also discuss
                what it feels like to converse with someone who does few
                of the positive behaviors listed. To illustrate the effects of
                bad habits, the group can sketch a cartoon-like picture of
                someone who has poor listening skills. Students can also set
                goals to acquire one or more of the good listening habits and
                commit these to writing in their agendas or journals.

Assessing My Listening Skills

Check any of these items that you specifically recall doing in the last two weeks of classes.

_____1.   Told another person what I liked about his or her ideas, specifically citing one or two of them.

_____2.   Maintained eye contact with the person speaking.

_____3.   Paid full attention to others' thoughts and words.

_____4.   Helped someone else join a discussion.

_____5.   Made a note about something I remembered I needed to do while the speaker was talking.

_____6.   Encouraged someone to share his or her feelings openly.

_____7.   Offered a helpful suggestion to others after asking permission.

_____8.   Sketched the speaker in a quick drawing.

_____9.   Asked another person in our group for help.

_____10. Explained my own ideas clearly, without putting others down.

_____11. Did not force my own opinions on the person speaking.

_____12. Paraphrased others' ideas to check for understanding.

_____13. Was sensitive to others' need to participate, so did not to take up much of the group's time.

_____14. Doodled on my agenda.

_____15. Noted the brand of the polo shirt the speaker was wearing and that at least one other classmate had on a similar brand but another color.

6. I Heard It Through the Grapevine ◼

Purpose:
To provide practice in listening carefully and passing on information correctly.

Materials:
Prepare six or more message cards. Use those suggested below or ones you create.

Time:
30 minutes.

Directions:
Arrange the group in a circle or line. The leader starts with a message on one of the cards that is whispered word for word to the first listener then whispered to each successive student. The final student repeats out loud what he or she heard, and this is compared with the original. The leader should be one of those involved in this activity.

Then after a second or third message is transmitted in this way, follow this variation: Select five students as participants and send four of them out of the room to wait in the hall. The student who has remained in the room (#1) is read a message from a printed card. One of the students is then called back into the room, and the first student repeats the message as she or he remembered it. A third student is then called back into the room, and the second student then tells him or her the message. The activity proceeds in this manner until the last student has received the message and repeated what he or she has heard. This method permits the rest of the group to hear how the message changes as it is relayed. Five volunteers might try to do a better job. Let them.

Discuss with the group the factors that caused the message to end up differently from the original and what helped the message to be successfully repeated each time. Is the articulation of the one speaking as much of a problem as the hearing of the recipient?

In the days ahead, when information is being shared, remind the students of what they learned from the grapevine experience.

Sample Messages

1. I'm having a birthday party at my house on Thursday, January 27, at 4:00 p.m. Can you come?

2. My telephone number is 473-5968, but I seldom use it.

3. Henry Weathersmith lives at 325 Wabash Avenue in Apartment #12.

4. Three of the best movies ever made are *Happy Feet, The Freedom Writers,* and *Polar Express,* according to one source.

5. Georgia has 159 counties, a large number even for a state relatively large in land area.

6. South Africa is said to be the only country with a capital not located on an important body of water.

7. Rescue at Sea 🅖

Purpose: To demonstrate the need for good communication—and the difficulties in achieving it—while having fun.

Materials: You'll need an open space, a gym or a field, and a blindfold.

Time: 15–25 minutes.

Directions: The participants all have a specific role to play. Identify individuals to play these roles: a blindfolded swimmer, a brave rescuer, two buoys bobbing upon the sea, two rocks just below the surface, and a floating jelly fish. The rest of the participants form two lines to represent jagged seaside cliffs.

The two lines of cliff representatives face each other about eight feet apart. The swimmer stands at one end of the lines, the rescuer at the other. The various obstacles can be placed anywhere between the two lines. The two lines make the sounds of a stormy sea. The buoys will clang, the rocks make the sound of pounding waves, but the jellyfish is silent.

The rescuer standing on the shore gives directions to the swimmer as she tries to make her way through the sea. Because of all the other noises, the rescuer has to be loud and clear while giving instructions, and the swimmer must listen. If the swimmer hits an obstacle, the leader takes her back to the starting position and she tries again. Once she has completed the course successfully, both rescuer and swimmer are replaced by others, and the game is repeated. Discuss what conditions are needed for good communication to occur.

8. Proverbs and Quotes ▪

Purpose: To provide an opportunity to recall and reflect on aspects of our history and culture while also getting the group to know one another better.

Materials: Enough "proverb cards" for every two students. The facilitator should write a number of famous quotes or proverbs that reflect the values of our society or some significant event in our history on 3" x 5" index cards. On one card write the beginning of the proverb or quote and on another write the completion of the phrase.

Directions: Shuffle the index cards, and with the deck's cards face down, have every participant draw one. Let everyone read the cards silently. Then tell them that somewhere in the room there is someone with the other part of the quotation or proverb. No talking or whispering is allowed as students mill about pointing and gesturing, trying to find their partners. When everyone has paired up, partners share their quotes and tell as much as they remember about its origin. Others chime in with their thoughts, and the leader then uses his or her judgment as to how much further to extend the discussion and the history lesson—it may be a teachable moment.

Some possible quotes:
- As Maine goes, so goes the nation.

- 54/40 or fight.

- One if by land, two if by sea.

- Ask not what your country can do for you, but what you can do for your country.

- A penny saved is a penny earned.

- I like Ike.

9. The In-Crowd ⓖ

Purpose: To enable students to think as anthropologists, analyze speech, and consider the ways that they may be excluding others through speech.

Materials: None necessary.

Time: 20 plus minutes.

Directions: The leader tells the students that all groups convey who is in "the in-crowd" and who is "out of it" by speech. The leader should then write the following dialogue on a whiteboard or overhead for students to translate.

> AISI, it's TEOTWAWKI ☺
> IYSS

(This is "text speak" for "As I see it, it's the end of the world as we know it" —a smiley face indicates exaggeration. The capital letters indicate "yelling." IYSS means "if you say so.")

Ask students to talk in pairs or triads about who is likely to be able to translate the dialogue and who would be unlikely to be able to do so. Also ask them to consider what it says about a person who could not translate the dialogue. Then they should compare and contrast the cultural aspects or values of the people as suggested by the type of speech used. (For instance, text speak is short, abbreviated, happens frequently, is enhanced by technology, and can be about less significant information; while people who don't use "text speak" may have wordier dialogue, talk less frequently, but have longer conversations. Using text speak might show a value of speed and being "up to the minute" while the other speech shows sluggishness and being "out of it.") Students should discuss in the small groups and then come up with a group list of all the ways they signify someone is "in" and someone is "out." They can also discuss ways to bring outsiders into a group by sharing speech. Finally, they should be asked to consider how inclusive they are of other members of the group or team and to think of other organizations where they may be inadvertently excluding others. An extension might be for students to write "text speak" to stump the leader.

10. Noteworthy News **G**

Purpose: To develop listening skills and get to know classmates better.

Materials: No special equipment is needed.

Time: 10 minutes.

Directions: Have the students form pairs, preferably on a Monday morning, and sit facing each other. Student A will describe his or her weekend. Then Student B will repeat what was heard, and Student A tells how well Student B did. Students then switch roles. Consider offering the opportunity for anyone to share something learned that might be of interest to others. Emphasize how articulate one needs to be as well as how carefully one has to listen.

11. Do You See What I'm Saying? ▮

Purpose: To develop participants' mathematical and spatial abilities as well as demonstrate the need for clear communication.

Materials: Participants need pencil and paper or stiff cards. Using colored pencils or markers, makes the activity more of a challenge (particularly if one can't use the names of the colors).

Directions: You can first demonstrate this to the group with a partner or have students go right to work in pairs. Ask each student to draw a geometric figure in a few seconds but not show it. Then have students form pairs sitting back-to-back. One student looks at his figure and carefully describes it to his partner while the partner tries to draw the geometric figure from his directions. Partners then change roles. Trying a second round is a possibility, or have one successful team demonstrate how to do it. The whole group discusses those strategies that aid in communication—and those that prevent us from "getting the picture"—and consider the applications in the classroom.

12. Photography G

Purpose: To demonstrate how individuals have different perceptions of the same scene.

Materials: No special equipment is needed; however the activity should be completed in a gym or field so that pairs can move about in a wide-open space.

Time: 20 minutes.

Directions: The participants are divided into pairs, with one assigned initially as the "camera" and one as the "photographer." "Cameras" close their eyes and are led by their partners, the photographers, to different objects or landscapes selected to be photographed. The photographers line up the cameras and then tap the cameras on the shoulder, a sign to open their eyes and take a picture. After only two or three seconds, the cameras must close their eyes and be led to the next scene. Members take three of four pictures before switching roles. After each has fulfilled both roles, the pairs discuss their perceptions and what might account for any differences. The point should be made that having varying perspectives allows for a more complete, though often different picture. Have students connect the experience to communication.

13. Who Am I? G

Purpose: To assist students in developing an understanding of human uniqueness and the implications for them personally and for the group.

Materials: To complete the activity you will need an ink pad, manila paper, scissors, and 3"x 5" index cards. If you display the work you will also need some type of adhesive.

Time: 40 to 50 minutes.

Directions: Open with the questions, "What does it mean to be unique?" and "How is each person special?" Then give participants the manila paper and allow them to cut the paper in any shape or form they choose. Students then individually make their thumbprint on the Manila paper, using the ink pad. Finally, using their imagination, the students should make a picture with their thumbprints and personalize the drawing by writing, "I am unique because..." You can post these on a wall.

Initiate the discussion by stating: "You are unique. There has never been anyone like you and there will never be again. Is that good, bad, or what? Do you agree? What are some implications of the statement?" After some discussion ask three or four people to summarize the sessions on uniqueness.

You may want to consider this variation: Ask each student to make a thumbprint on an index card. Shuffle the cards. Tell each person to find his or her thumbprint. Give the group about three minutes to identify each person's print and then say, "Now we will fingerprint your thumb again to see whether you were right." Discuss how they found their thumbprints.

14. Twist and Roll G

Purpose: To help young adolescents express some of the difficult things, both positive and negative, that they could say to each other.

Materials: A bag of mini-Tootsie Rolls™, a bag of mini-twist pretzels, and a pack of index cards.

Time: 15–30 minutes.

Directions: You may inform participants in advance what this activity will involve or initiate it without advance notice. On Thursday or Friday and after a sufficient amount of time for observation, have students sit in a circle so that they can see each other and think about those things fellow students have done well during the week or annoying things they have done. Go around the circle and ask individuals to share some recollections. For each compliment offered, a Tootsie Roll is given to the teammate who was responsible for the action; and, in like manner, for each criticism a pretzel is handed over. Participants can give out as many rolls as they'd like (unlimited compliments) but may only give out one complaint per student (pretzel twist). The group should ensure that each person receives a compliment.

After you have gone through this exercise a time or two, you can close the activity by handing each participant two sheets of paper or index cards with the words "One thing I am going to start doing" written on one and "One thing I am going to stop doing" written on the other. Each person completes with a written response. At a subsequent meeting, students can review how their commitments to start and stop behaviors are going. One option is to close the session by having the group form a circle with a trash can in the center. Students read aloud their "start" statements and toss the other statement into the trash can without revealing it to the group.

15. Agitation G

Purpose: To provide an experience for group goal setting during frenzied action.

Materials: An open, indoor space and enough balloons for two for each person. A stopwatch or a watch with a second hand.

Directions: Participants form a circle, and two balloons are given to each person. Each person inflates and knots his or her balloons, keeping one and putting the other in a pile near the timekeeper. The designated timekeeper reviews the rules: 1) At the signal each person is to knock a balloon into the air and keep it aloft—no resting it on objects or using static electricity to affix it to a wall. 2) Every five seconds the timekeeper will loft another balloon into the mix, adding to the agitation. New balloons become the group's responsibility to keep aloft. 3) Penalties will be noted each time a balloon comes in contact with anything other than air—desks, people, the floor, etc. 4) When the group has amassed five penalties, time will be noted and the round called to an end. 5) Give the group the opportunity to strategize between rounds (about four or five rounds is usually good) and to determine what would be considered a really good time.

Afterwards, have the group discuss any goal setting that went into the activity and how the members went about meeting the goal. Did having someone assume leadership help or hinder the group in reaching its goals?

16. Full Circle G T

Purpose: To build more trust within a group already pretty much "together."

Materials: No special equipment is necessary, only an area free of obstacles.

Directions: Warn participants how seriously the activity should be taken. All participants stand in a tight circle in a "ready to catch" position, shoulder to shoulder. This means that each person has a foot firmly planted for support bracing and hands out, palms up, with the fingers slightly bent (as in volleyball). One volunteer stands in the middle of the circle in the "ready to fall" position, which means arms at side and stiffened body. The person in the center calls out "Ready to fall." The group responds "Ready to catch." "Falling." "Catching." These safety aspects are important to follow even if they seem repetitive. The participant in the center falls backward into the human circle. The group works together to pass the participant gently and completely around the circle, and then stand him or her up again. After everyone who would like to gets a chance to fall, discuss the feelings of fallers and catchers.

17. Group Dynamics Ⓖ

Purpose: To provide an opportunity for a group to consider how far it
                has come in becoming a fully effective working group.

Materials: A copy of Tuckman's Four Stages of Group Development.

Time: 20–40 minutes.

Directions: Share the handout with the group, and after members take
                a few minutes to read it, open discussion. At what stage is
                this group? How can we move to the next stage? This activity
                works well when the group is still coming together and then
                can be repeated some time later.

Stages of Group Development

Bruce Tuckman* (1965) viewed the development of a group as having four stages: *1) forming, 2) storming, 3) norming,* and *4) performing.*

Forming is the stage when the group first comes together. Everybody is polite, and conflict is seldom voiced directly. Since the grouping is new, individuals are guarded in their own opinions and generally reserved. One or two dominant leaders will risk being seen as brash, and the group looks to them for leadership and tends to follow them.

Storming is the next stage; and as the term suggests, there is a great deal of fighting over every point. Personal differences emerge and become irritations. Emotions come to the surface and drive the group. Most importantly, very little communication occurs, since no one is listening; and some are unwilling to talk openly. With all of the clashing, it is easy for gossip to emerge and take place outside of the time when the group is together. This is a time of great challenge for many groups, particularly if they are unaware of this expected stage.

This is followed by the **norming** stage. At this stage the infighting subsides, and a new spirit of cooperation is evident. Because of this security, all members, not just vocal ones, express their own viewpoints, which are discussed frankly with the whole group. The most significant improvement is that people start to listen to each other. The ways in which the group will complete its work are considered, established, accepted, and practiced as the group becomes a cohesive unit.

The highest level is called **performing.** This is the culmination, when the group has settled on a system that allows free and frank exchange of views and a high degree of support by the group for each other and its own decisions. The group has a sense of pride and empowerment. The members are collaborative rather than politely cooperative and there is collective responsibility for the process as well as the product. This is the level to which a team or an advisory group should aim.

---

*Tuckman, B. (1965). Developmental sequence in small groups. *Psychological Bulletin, 63* (6), 384-399.

Also see http://gom.sagepub.com/cgi/content/abstract/2/4/419

18. Building Self-Respect G

Purpose: To learn to deal with "killer" comments, those put-downs that cause a great deal of anxiety and strife in the middle years.

Materials: Provide a couple of movie or television clips for this exercise or a real example you witnessed. You also will need a large board to list negative incidences, ways to avoid negative talk, and to display agreed-upon norms.

Time: The first part can be completed in 20 minutes, while the follow-up assignment and creation of norms will take at least 40 minutes.

Directions: Start with an example of your own or share a film clip. Then have participants share examples of a put-down they have experienced or one from television shows they have seen. List the incidents on the board. Have the group discuss how the put-down made the person feel. Have individuals also try to get at the feelings of the one who is doing the putting down. Discuss the cognitive and emotional reasons that adolescents get mired in "put-down" talk. Have learners suggest ways to avoid negative talk.

After the discussion has seemed to run its course, give an assignment that for one week each person is to keep track of put-downs given, received, or witnessed. Regroup and set personal goals to significantly reduce the number of put-downs given or witnessed. Finally the group should create the norms to which the members will adhere. Discuss such things as confidentiality, staying on task, being open to change, and embracing diversity. Finally, everyone needs to agree to follow the norms in order to be a member of the group in good standing.

19. Times I've Deserved a Pat on the Back ◘

Purpose: To help participants recognize their strengths and develop a
                  positive self-concept.

Materials: Copies of the worksheet "Times I've Deserved a Pat on
                  the Back."

Time: 30 minutes.

Directions: Distribute the worksheet for students to complete. After
                  8–10 minutes, have students choose a partner to exchange
                  achievements and discuss how these achievements show
                  their growing maturity and why they are worthy of recognition.
                  Lastly they should each add one other item to the list not
                  already considered.

Times I've Deserved a Pat on the Back

We need to give ourselves recognition. If we wait for it to come from others, we feel resentful when it doesn't; and when it does, we may not believe it. It is not what others say to us that counts. We all love praise, but have you ever noticed how quickly the glow from a compliment wears off? When we compliment ourselves, the glow stays with us longer. It is still good to hear it from others, but it doesn't matter so much if we have already heard it from ourselves.

Take a look at the statements below. You've probably done each of these things at one time or another but have forgotten about it. (We tend to remember our failures and forget our strengths). Choose four of the eight statements and be ready to describe the situation and what you did. Then be prepared to share one of your successes with the class.

1. I tried something I thought would be difficult.

2. I avoided putting someone down even though I felt like it.

3. I stuck with a job that was hard to do, and I finally finished it.

4. I avoided making excuses or blaming someone else for what I did.

5. I told the truth even though I was afraid I'd get in trouble.

6. I didn't go along with what others were doing because I thought it was wrong.

7. I controlled my temper in a difficult situation.

8. I have made a concerted effort to get along better with someone in my family.

20. The Unit 🄶

Purpose: To promote the development of communication skills and
             build self-confidence. This can be is a memorable experience
             for large or small groups, but it requires a certain confidence
             level, and it is important to establish a serious atmosphere.

Materials: Materials are identified in the directions below. Ample open
             space is needed, indoors or outside.

Time: 25 minutes.

Directions: Distribute objects e.g., balls, bowling pins, cones, foam
             noodles, even classroom furniture, etc. as obstacles
             throughout the designated area. Participants operate as pairs.
             One person is blindfolded (or really keeps eyes closed) and
             cannot talk (optional). The other person can see and talk, but
             cannot enter the field or touch the person. The challenge is
             for each blindfolded person to navigate from one side of the
             field to the other, avoiding the obstacles by listening to the
             verbal instructions of his or her partner. Decide in advance
             on the penalty for hitting an obstacle. It could be a restart,
             or time penalty, or a tally of hits, but without penalty. It can
             help participants if it is suggested that they develop a unique
             communication system; or when they swap roles, you can
             offer participants some review and planning time to define
             their communication method once this need becomes
             obvious.

             To enhance safety, you can monitor the playing area to help
             prevent collisions. Allow participants to swap roles several
             times until a sense of skill and competence in being able
             to guide a partner through the blockages develops. This
             experience provides the opportunity to discuss reliance on
             a partner, effective communication, and the importance of
             dependability for becoming a unit.

21. Traditions ⏣

Purpose: To build cohesiveness in a group.

Materials: None needed.

Time: 25 minutes or more.

Directions: Each member of the group shares a family tradition that has some personal importance. For instance, a holiday tradition (we always decorate the tree on December 20th after supper), weekly routines (Saturday mornings I do household chores before I can go out), or activities idiosyncratic to a particular individual (my dad insists on having applesauce and makes rice to go with pork chops). These are placed on a large poster. The group discusses the value of traditions to different cultures, social groups for creating group identity, and helping them persevere in difficult times.

Finally the group should create and implement a tradition, routine, or identifying idiosyncrasy it will embrace for the life of this group. This might be a making a banner with the team name and logo on it, recognizing "Our Student of the Week," engaging in "Noteworthy News" each Monday, or even always giving the group a standing ovation to start its meetings.

22. Labeling 🅖

Purpose: To consider stereotyping and value judgments

Materials: No materials needed.

Time: Variable, but at least 25–30 minutes.

Directions: Select a number of classifications by which judgments are made and by which people can be separated. For instance, "height," "gender," and "musical talent" are a few that are relatively benign; but categories such as "intelligence," "weight," or "skin color" can have quite a sting associated with them. Separate the group using one criterion, asking those named to move away from the remaining members. Then have members determine the criteria, discussing the implications of being in the "tall" or "short" group. Then, separate the group on the basis of another criterion. Finally assign one of the conditions, for instance "short" as "good" and "tall" as "bad," with the "good" condition allowing for extra privileges such as free time for socializing.

Go through this a few times with different criteria and with a different condition being labeled "good." For instance, "musical talent" might be "good" while "language talent" would be the "bad" condition. Have students write their responses to being labeled "bad" or "good" by criteria over which they had no control (such as eye color) and by which others judged them positively or negatively. Finally have a group discussion about various reactions to the activities while students explore the notions of stereotyping, prejudice, and value judgments. The "judging" phase can be carried out for a longer period of time for groups that are further along in their own emotional development.

23. Walk a Mile ▣

Purpose: To develop students' abilities to understand others' perspectives and to learn not to judge those from whom they differ.

Materials: Materials as described below need to be prepared ahead of time.

Time: 60–75 minutes.

Directions: Divide students into small groups (3–5) that are a cross-section representing to the degree possible the diversity that exists in the total group. Create packets to distribute, one per group, that contain pictures, artifacts, and information about a distinct geographical section of the world such as the Middle East or the Pacific Islands. The packet should *not* contain pictures of people or dwellings, as these will be factors in the questions the students consider.

Instruct the small groups to consider the information in their packets and respond to the following prompts:

1) Describe the types of homes the people would need to live in the region and provide support for your reasoning.

2) Describe the clothing you would expect people residing in this area to wear and provide support for your reasoning.

3) Finally describe the strengths such people would likely develop as a result of where they live and provide support for your reasoning.

The small groups present their work to the total group, followed by a whole-class discussion about the advantages and disadvantages of living in each area. Alert the group to look for stereotypes voiced during the discussion. Finally help students see how their own background and experiences influence the ways they consider people and places different from themselves.

24. Values Auction ∎

Purpose:
To help students consider what they value at this point in their lives, and why.

Materials:
Enough "play" money to provide each person with $500 and a list of 20 items for auction. Auction items might include popularity, integrity, intelligence, a week's supply of my favorite food, world travel, good health, self-confidence, athletic ability, ideal weight, latest cell phone, or a daylong date with a favorite celebrity.

Time:
30 minutes.

Directions:
Distribute exactly $500 to each person. Then distribute a list of about 20 items that you have developed for the auction, including values, actions, aspirations, or items that advisees might desire. Explain how an auction works and give students some time to consider items on which they would like to bid. You act as the auctioneer, putting up items—not necessarily in the order they appeared on the list.

Once the auction has been conducted, review those items that seemed in great demand and compare them to those that were less coveted. Let individuals share their strategies, the reasons for their choices. Also discuss why different people desire different items and how the money was used in different ways (one expensive item vs. several less expensive ones). Discuss the dilemma that exists when one or two want a particular item. Finally, ask students to write in their journals what, if anything, their choices reveal about themselves and others and to speculate about how their parents would have participated in the auction.

25. Becoming Me ∎

Purpose: To discuss self-identification.

Materials: Each member of the group will need a copy of the survey below, with some additions you select.

Time: 25 minutes or more.

Directions: Participants should take two or three minutes to complete the short survey and then discuss their answers to gain an understanding of adolescence as a time for self-identification and validation of differences. This is likely to take longer—and should—if the members take this opportunity to "air out" many of their concerns related to adolescent-adult relationships.

SURVEY

I like to wear the same kind of clothes as my family.

My younger sister/brother/relative acts just like me.

I like to spend my free time the same way as does my family.

I use the same kind of language as my family.

My family generally shares my taste in music.

The friends of the adults in my family are just like my friends.

If we were out in public and you saw us from the back, you might not be able to tell me from my parent.

My family's feelings about tattoos, hair styles, and makeup are the same as mine.

My younger sisters/brothers/cousins and I laugh about the same things.

26. Trust Building ⒼⓉ

Purpose: To help students be vulnerable to teammates and to build trust among members of the group.

Materials: A gym or open field as well as blindfolds.

Time: 20 minutes or less.

Directions: One volunteer stands at the end of the gym facing the opposing court. He is blindfolded and puts his palms out in front of him about chest high as a protective measure. He then jogs slowly across the gym floor at a steady pace. The other members of the group are spread out across the back wall (and a couple closer to the start point in case the jogger is disoriented) and remain silent as the jogger approaches. They call out "Stop!" only if the jogger is in danger of colliding into someone or something. Give each participant and opportunity to jog. Group members then discusses concerns as a blindfolded jogger and their commitments as protectors.

27. Color me ...? ∎

Purpose: To investigate the meaning of "race."

Materials: Use the Internet to find information to share.

Time: 75 minutes.

Directions: This activity can begin with a biological explanation of "race," which differs from the older social construct based on a classification system by skin color and physical attributes that was determined centuries ago. Today's accepted biological explanation is that skin color and other physical attributes are adaptations that occurred over time in response to the environment where people and their ancestors lived. For about 50 years scientists have looked at changes in DNA structure to determine how people are alike and different.

Assign pairs of students to investigate the meaning, use, and synonyms for the colors black, white, tan, red, yellow, when applied to people. The group should compile a single list and review how the various terms are applied elsewhere (black gold, white collar job, yellow journalism, redneck, "to tan" is to give a spanking). The group should consider if some colors are generally held in positive regard, while others often have a negative association. Discuss whether people perceive color differences and when this begins to happen. Ask if there is any relationship to the meaning of the words and stereotyping. Finally, talk about what the connotations of the colors, if used to describe a person, might do to a person's developing self-image.

If the group is sophisticated enough and you feel equipped to discuss the topic you might ask advisees to relate when and where they became cognizant of different races or their own race. You could also inform students about theories of racial identity formation.

28. 1-2-1 G

Purpose: To emphasize paying attention to nonverbal cues.

Materials: No materials necessary.

Time: 15 minutes.

Directions: Each person should pick a partner who is not a friend and
                may be different from himself or herself in some way and
                stand about 10 feet apart. Then each person makes eye
                contact with his or her partner and slowly walks closer and
                closer until the comfort zone has been breached. The pairs
                should hold this position for a few moments until the advisor
                allows them to relax. Then discuss the comfort zone and how it
                may differ in certain circumstances. Have individuals tell how
                they felt when their personal space was infiltrated as well as
                share their feelings about maintaining the invasion for a little
                while. See if there were more similarities or differences about
                interpretations as to how close "close enough" is.

                Discuss as well other aspects of body language and other
                nonverbal cues commonly used by teachers and students,
                such as how one positions his arms when standing or when
                one intentionally avoids eye contact.

29. Free Write ∎

Purpose: To allow advisees some individual thinking time and free
            writing time while assessing the advisory program. While this
            activity is specifically designed for an advisory program, it can
            be adapted to use with a class or some student group such as
            student council.

Materials: Only writing materials are necessary.

Time: 10–15 minutes.

Directions: Use any of the following prompts to guide the free-write:
            — Is judging something good or a bad thing a wise
              thing to do? Why?
            — Have you ever judged someone incorrectly?
              Have you ever been judged incorrectly?
            — Do you tend to be a follower or a leader?
              How could you become more of the other?
            — What activities in advisory have been beneficial for
              you to complete? Why?
            — What activities in advisory have been easy for you
              to complete? Why?
            — What activities in advisory have not been beneficial
              for you to complete? Why?
            — What activities in advisory have not been easy for you
              to complete? Why?
            — Do you feel that your group is building trust
              among its members?
            — Do you feel that the members of your advisory group
              are more alike or more different from each other?
              In what ways?
            — Can you design an activity that you think your group
              should try?
            — What will you remember most from participating in
              advisory with this group?
            — Who will you remember most from this group
              and why?

30. Assessment ▣

Purpose: To ascertain what students are learning following the completion of a series of lessons.

Materials: Note cards and poster materials.

Time: Up to 50 minutes.

Directions: Participants each receive four blank cards and are asked to put four different responses to the question, "What were main concepts or learning points of the material we just covered?" Give them about three to five minutes to complete the exercise, then collect the cards, shuffle them, and randomly deal three cards to each learner. (Note: If desired, you can make up four cards of your own that are philosophically at odds with the principles presented. That is, play the devil's advocate.)

Ask everyone to read the cards received and then to arrange them in order of personal preference. Place the extra cards on the table and allow participants to replace the cards in their hand that they do not like because they don't represent a main point just learned. Next, have each student exchange at least one card with another student.

After about three minutes, form participants into teams of three or four and ask each team to select the three cards it likes the best. Give them time to choose, then have them create and present a graphic poster to reflect the final three cards. To what degree were the cards selected reflective of the material presented?

31. It's All in the 'Tude ⒼⒾ

Purpose: To demonstrate how focusing on bad things depletes energy levels, while focusing on good things raises energy levels.

Materials: Participants for the discussion is all you need.

Time: At least 50 minutes for completion, but it can be broken into parts.

Directions: Divide participants into two groups and place them in two areas so one group is not conscious of the other group. The first group will discuss among themselves a bad school experience, such as a bad environment, relationship with a teacher, or content that seemed like a foreign language. The experience can either be in the present or past. Ask students not to use names. Allow each person an opportunity to speak before going to round two. Expect them to work on this exercise for about 10 to 15 minutes. Have them jot down a brief highlight or description of each bad experience on the flip chart.

The second group will discuss among themselves a good school experience, such as a great teacher, working environment, or good learning activities. The experience can either be in the present or past. Again tell students not to use names. Allow each person an opportunity to speak before going to round two. Work on this exercise for about 10 to 15 minutes and have them jot down a brief highlight or description of each good experience on the flip chart.

Monitor the two groups. You should see a difference between the two groups, happy faces vs. glum faces, excitement vs. "let's get this exercise over with," bright flip charts vs. dull flip charts—evidences of a marked distinction between the energized group (discussing good experiences) and the drained group (discussing bad experiences). Make notes of what you see. You might even consider videotaping to use as a part of the debriefing.

When the time period is over, bring the two groups together to discuss their bad and good experiences. Have each group give a brief presentation of bad and good experiences. The "bad experiences group" goes first. (NOTE: their short presentation might start affecting the second group.)
Next, have the second group highlight some good school experiences. When the second group is about finished, point out the marked differences between the two groups if they aren't already apparent. Ask them how they felt while they were discussing their bad or good experiences. Point out that it is hard to stay energized when you focus on the negative.

National Middle School Association

Since 1973, National Middle School Association (NMSA) has been the voice for those committed to the education and well-being of young adolescents and is the only national association dedicated exclusively to middle level youth.

NMSA's members are principals, teachers, central office personnel, professors, college students, parents, community leaders, and educational consultants in the United States, Canada, and 46 other countries. A major advocacy effort is Month of the Young Adolescent. This October celebration engages a wide range of organizations to help schools, families, and communities celebrate and honor young adolescents for their contributions to society.

NMSA offers publications, professional development services, and events for middle level educators seeking to improve the education and overall development of 10- to 15-year-olds. In addition to the highly acclaimed *Middle School Journal, Middle Ground* magazine, and *Research in Middle Level Education Online,* we publish more than 100 books on every facet of middle level education. Our landmark position paper, *This We Believe,* is recognized as the premier statement outlining the vision of middle level education.

Membership is open to anyone committed to the education of young adolescents. Visit **www.nmsa.org** or call **1-800-528-NMSA** for more information.

CPSIA information can be obtained
at www.ICGtesting.com
Printed in the USA
FFOW02n2126050816
26524FF